ONE HUNDRED PENNIES

ONE HUNDRED PENNIES

The Importance of Small Business in a Healthy Economy

MICHAEL S. ROBINSON

Copyright © 2013 by Michael S. Robinson

Published by Microbin
39 Broadway
Suite 2440
New York, NY 10006

Manufactured in the United States of America

ISBN 978-0-9887877-0-4
Library of Congress Catalog Card No. 2012924151

0 9 8 7 6 5 4 3 2 1

Cover and interior design by Cindy LaBreacht

TO MOM

CONTENTS

INTRODUCTION

M y pioneering idea for rejuvenating the main engine of the
American economy, i .e., small business, is the result of two
events that occurred recently in my life. The first was a White
House meeting that never happened, followed by invitations to
speak at various political county engagements across the State
of New York. Along my journey, I had the opportunity to speak
with many small-business owners and witness the economic
devastation on a widespread basis, which was both jarring and
an eye-opener.

In 2009 President Obama was planning a nationwide jobs
summit, and John Coyle, an official at the Department of Commerce, was asked to select two businesses to represent New
York State. My company, New York Staffing Services, Inc., was
one of those chosen. Our reputation for excellence in the New
York business community, combined with over two decades of
consistent growth, made us an easy choice. Still it was quite an
honor, given the number of businesses in New York City alone.

The opportunity to discuss my ideas with the President was
thrilling, to say the least. I imagined presenting my ideas on how
to correct and improve the existing situation—wherein an excess

of jobs were being outsourced and an astonishing number of small businesses sacrificed to both the big corporate engine and a rapidly evolving global economy—and get our economy back on track. My action plan was primarily devised to help thousands of small businesses nationwide—to solidify and strengthen their positions, thus jump-starting the economy.

I anticipated some initial resistance. Any plan focused on small-business creation is too often met with derision and yawns, or worse yet characterized as "cliché" by know-it-all cynics. But there's no getting away from the fact that clichés are based on truth, however overstated across time. The derision fast disappears as soon as a solution is presented that works. What remains the optimum tool for revitalizing the U.S. economy? Small business…the opposite of where all the attention has been since the economic meltdown of 2009.

Alas, not long after my exciting White House invitation, I learned (like many a laid-off worker) that I'd been dismissed… not from my job, but from the guest list, which had had to be trimmed. Disappointed? Yes. Dissuaded? No! The ideas inspired by the presidential invitation had begun to bear fruit. I couldn't let go of the plan I'd developed; over time I continued to expound and expand on it, integrating its principles and practices. Soon I had envisioned a direct and targeted action plan with a number of critical components, including:

➤ Encouraging partnerships between large and small businesses focused on solutions to the current crisis.
➤ Government incentives for businesses to bring back jobs to the United States.
➤ Research and development to encourage invention.
➤ Promoting small-business clusters across the country.
➤ Simplifying interstate commerce.
➤ PPP (private-public partnerships).

- ➤ Providing investment incentives to local banks, so that small businesses can gain easier access to funds.
- ➤ Creating the National Centralized Business Resources Center to provide efficient information for doing business within a particular state, and streamlining the application process.

Eventually I found myself the author of more than a mere presentation; it was a fully fledged treatise—virtually a manifesto. I decided to publish it as a book.

I DREW MY TITLE from an eye-opening statistic. For every one hundred pennies generated from our Gross Domestic Product (GDP), almost *sixty cents* comes from small business, according to the Department of Commerce. So why does it seem as though small businesses are treated as an afterthought by both our government and big businesses, especially during difficult economic times like the Great Recession? While billions of dollars were generously handed to large corporations in Troubled Asset Relief Program (TARP) bailouts, small businesses were left to navigate the turbulent waters of our economy with neither a paddle nor a GPS. In September 2010 the Obama Administration passed the Small Business Jobs Act, designed to throw a lifeline to sinking ships, but it was ineffective and provided few necessary solutions. In fact, it was a classic case of too little, too late, since thousands of small businesses had already closed their doors permanently, while many others were hemorrhaging losses en route to bankruptcy.

Thus unemployment continued to climb, consumer spending was at a standstill, and as a result our economy continued to struggle. The giants, however, were still making huge profits and squeezing every drop of profit from the small-business communities which served their needs. Our government did not provide any effective solutions to move our country through a stagnant economy, hoping that things would fall back into place automatically. But this was no ordinary recession and the consequences reverberated in many towns, counties, and cities all across the nation. Valuable solutions were provided by the government that in healthy economic conditions would have been perfect, such as rebuilding our country's infrastructure: highways, airports, bridges, etc. This was expected to create thousands of jobs, all of which were necessary. But the reality is that government does not create jobs; the private sector creates jobs. And in a difficult economy a rapid upswing in private-sector hiring is essential to getting things back on track. The fact of the matter is that small businesses are the largest job creators in the United States. Government's role must be to provide effective tools, easily accessible resources, and information to small businesses, so that we can stimulate and encourage this vital sector of our economy to grow and prosper.

One Hundred Pennies has been written to simplify complex ideas by shedding light on the value of small businesses to a healthy U.S. economy. With my more than twenty years of entrepreneurial experience, having built corporations and hired thousands of employees over the years, I've dealt with the challenges of navigating my company though difficult economic times, including the tragedy of 9/11, and yet have remained successful. My goal is to put things into perspective by outlining the main economic problems that stagnate our economy, as well as provide basic solutions that will get our nation back on track, from a small-business standpoint.

The United States economy is a multifaceted one, driven by many engines. The main engine that propels the economy forward is consumer spending, which one could say actively recycles money. However, for this to happen consumers need to have good-paying jobs, and businesses need to provide products and services that attract those consumers to spend their earnings.

This healthy flow of money further promotes business growth, creates new jobs, and generates higher tax revenue that allows the government to function more effectively when managed wisely. The result is a stronger economy that provides more efficient social services, a fair legal and regulatory system, a strong military, and greater protection of our borders—well, at least ideally speaking. Small businesses play a vital role in not only facilitating this process but also contributing to the economic health of our nation.

Before we move forward I think it's important to clarify what a small business is so that we're all on the same page. The Small Business Administration (SBA) has established a definition. Ready? It goes like this:

1. Manufacturing: Maximum number of employees may range from 500 to 1500, depending on the type of product manufactured.
2. Wholesaling: Maximum number of employees may range from 100 to 500, depending on the particular product being provided.
3. Services: Annual receipts may not exceed $2.5 to $21.5 million, depending on the particular service being provided.
4. Retailing: Annual receipts may not exceed $5.0 to $21.0 million, depending on the particular product being provided.
5. General and Heavy Construction: General construction annual receipts may not exceed $13.5 to $17 million, depending on the type of construction.
6. Special Trade Construction: Annual receipts may not exceed $7 million.
7. Agriculture: Annual receipts may not exceed $0.5 to $9.0 million, depending on the agricultural product.[1]

I will make a bold statement by saying every one of today's large corporations that was started in the United States began as a small business. Think of Bill Gates starting his business in his father's garage a few decades ago…Starbucks emerging from a small café in Seattle…and the list goes on. The Small Business Administration refers to these as high-impact businesses, or gazelles. Not every small business turns into a gazelle, of course; in fact only a small percentage do, while some fail due to a variety of reasons. (We'll discuss gazelles in greater depth in Chapter Five.) However, the majority of small businesses that succeed are known as the backbone of our economy for many reasons. They hire the vast majority of Americans, register more patents, provide support for large corporations (including government), create the largest volume of new jobs in the United States, and provide the most innovate products/services to help move this country forward.

However, there is a struggle within many broad sectors of our economy that has led to several adverse turns of events, resulting in the economic downturn of the Great Recession. A struggle exists between small and big businesses, as the pressure to find cheaper global suppliers from big businesses has forced many small, regional businesses to rethink their business model, often having to close up shop when a global supplier is chosen over them. In addition, that struggle is even greater between businesses and government, which can often lead to economic dysfunction, especially during difficult economic times and in this rapidly evolving global economy. The struggle is often between the role of government in the business community and the role of business in providing services, products, and jobs to promote economic growth. The reality is that with regard to the economy, government provides legal protection, support, and incentives for businesses and in return, collects taxes and implements reasonable regulations. However, when taxes are too high and the regulations too restrictive, businesses find it more costly to grow, and as a result many consider staff reduction, outsourcing jobs, moving production to cheaper locations void of burdensome taxes and overregulation, or simply closing up shop. The end result is that we, the taxpayers, suffer the consequences as the United States loses its competitive edge in a rapidly evolving global economy, with countries like India and China swiftly gaining a strong foothold, having learned from our successes and capitalized on our failures.

SO WE'VE ESTABLISHED that small businesses are the fulcrum of the American economy, creating more jobs than larger corporations, inventing more products, registering more patents, generating more revenue from exports than large corporations nationwide, remaining on the cutting edge of innovation, and driving competition to higher levels. The end result is a consumer-driven economy where buyers want to spend and sellers make money, which increases tax revenue paid to our government, creating a complete interconnected circle wherein everyone benefits. Why then do we not have a stronger infrastructure to support small businesses that have the potential to succeed, yet are vulnerable due to complex economic swings?

Let me tell you a true story that encapsulates my point and shows what happens when a small business fails:

Danielle owned a prosperous public-relations firm in midtown Manhattan for fifteen years, with a staff comprising sixty-three employees in both New York and Chicago. The initial tidings of ill fortune appeared as follows: Longstanding clients requested PR firms with a global presence and thus began negotiating cheaper rates with a single supplier. Boutique firms like Danielle's found themselves losing contracts to national and global PR firms. While subcontracting with such firms was an option, it proved unprofitable—most major contractors kept the majority of business for themselves. Then the onset of the recession brought a loss in business. Now a strug-gling enterprise, Danielle's firm took a further hit from the high cost of corporate taxes in New York. Loans were unavail-able from banks (bailout beneficiaries) who refused to lend to small businesses. The Small Business Administration provided no support in terms of lending or guidance to keep the busi-ness open. Result? The business closed in June 2010, after a gradual downsizing of personnel over the previous four years.

The Great Recession and the rapidly changing global econ-omy have taken a terrible toll on small businesses in the US. The SBA admits that since the recession the volume of revenue generated from small businesses has fallen below the previous percent ratio of the GDP compared with larger corporations be-fore the recession began. Well of course it has—again proving my point. The SBA was formed to provide support and assis-tance to small businesses across the United States and has had a few success stories. But there are far too many small businesses that have fallen through the cracks, failures that could have been saved with better programs available. So what is the func-tion of the SBA and why was it unable to assist Danielle?

From my personal experience, the organization is ineffective, inflexible, obsolete, and unable to provide meaningful solutions for many small businesses in distress. How do I know this? By firsthand experience (which I will discuss at the end of Chapter Four), augmented by a multitude of discussions with hundreds of other small-business owners across the country.

Is this true across the board? No; the SBA can be a viable and more effective entity if streamlined and revamped.

Many small businesses rushed to commercial banks in the hope of securing a loan backed by the SBA, but were told that the banks weren't lending to small businesses at that time. Remember, these are the same banks that received billions of dollars in TARP bailouts from the government. So why were they not encouraged or supported by the government to provide financial assistance to small businesses backed by SBA programs? The SBA monitors and provides reporting data regarding small businesses that can be useful from a monitoring standpoint, but what good is that for the Danielles of the world who would have preferred to receive a helping hand rather than become a statistic for analysts to debate?

On a national scale, it's much more than a personal frustration: as I've noted, such small businesses are the veritable engine of the American economy. When they fail, the repercussions are widespread and progressively painful. The effects are detrimental to the communities they serve and to the economy as a whole. Multiply this scenario thousands of times across this nation, and suddenly the idea of billions of dollars in lost revenues and lost jobs become clearer. What has happened to the American economy in the past several years? Why does national unemployment continue to hover ominously at a high rate?

RECENTLY I WAS ABLE to tour several of the sixty-two counties that make up the great Empire State of New York. It was both alarming and disturbing to see how many ghost towns were left as a result of a lack of jobs and businesses. Streets were literally abandoned, with dozens of small businesses permanently closed due to a lack of industry to support these communities. During one of my trips to Buffalo, I met a young man by the name of Jesse who was returning home from a job interview in New York City. He sat next to me on the plane and we chatted for the majority of the trip. Jesse confided in me that he recently graduated from college at the age of twenty-one but could not find employment in his hometown. In fact the only job that was available to him was that of a lumberjack. Jesse wanted more from life, and his only recourse was to relocate to a city where the likelihood of employment in his chosen field was possible. Think of the thousands of graduating college students all across our country who, like Jesse, are unable to find jobs in the communities where their families have lived for generations. Instead they must migrate to bigger cities where the likelihood of finding employment is greater. As the demographics shift geographically, less vibrant communities are left with nothing to offer their remaining citizens, especially the younger generation, and pockets of economically unstable communities surface all across our great nation.

In outlining the crisis we are now facing as a country, I will show how the normal recession difficulties—such as unemployment, business failures, housing-price declines, and others—are eclipsed by the more serious issues of small-business failures, while outlining viable solutions to these problems. How? By proactively encouraging invention, creating a healthy economic climate that attracts and promotes business growth and development, simplifying interstate commerce, lowering taxes, reducing overregulation, and reforming government to run more efficiently, with clear benchmarks and a greater system of accountability.

A LITTLE ABOUT ME

Like one of our founding fathers, Alexander Hamilton, I was born and raised in the British Caribbean, but immigrated to the United States in my teens. In the early 1980s I arrived in the U.S. from the islands of St. Vincent and the Grenadines, having earned my GCE O and A Levels from the United Kingdom. I put myself through college while working full time on Wall Street—yes, with major banking institutions. I graduated from Brooklyn College in 1989 with a Bachelor of Science degree in Business Management and Finance, with a minor in Communications.

My résumé includes a 26-year career in business, finance, and management with over twenty years as an entrepreneur. In 1990 I opened New York Staffing Services, a successful firm with headquarters in the financial district that has employed thousands of people during the past twenty years. During that time we expanded our services across the country with additional offices in Tampa, Florida. In 2006 I created Microbin, a workforce capital-management firm developed as an Internet-based tool to streamline and manage the staffing process in large corporations worldwide. As you can see, the experience that informs my practical suggestions for overcoming the current crisis—a quarter-century of successful private-sector entrepreneurship—is broad and multidimensional. I have developed a vision that includes plans for permanent, beneficial changes that can achieve a more efficient U.S. economy in a rapidly changing world. It is a long-term strategic plan—one that benefits rather than destroys small business in particular.

In the following chapters, I will succinctly discuss our current underlying economic problems, which were brewing prior to the Great Recession; discuss viable solutions to strengthen the economy; and look at its future. My main focus is on small business, not because I'm a small-business owner but because I see the need for stronger, more deliberate input from government and big businesses versus the rhetoric I constantly hear. Then again, small-business owners must also unite and provide support for each other, using whatever tools are available to move their businesses forward. Complacency is never the answer to any problem. Small businesses can only survive by strategically adjusting to new economic paradigms.

Part One

PROBLEMS

1

HIDDEN PROBLEMS RATTLE
THE DEPTHS OF THE U.S. ECONOMY

Presently, we Americans find ourselves trapped in a vicious circle: using tax dollars for something that, however necessary, fails to accomplish its goal. The national debt, the deficit, whose numbers tick away furiously on lighted signs in the Big Apple, increases by the second. Does anyone know where the brakes are, or how to use them? The deficit grows as:

➤ Insufficient production and services nationwide result in insufficient tax revenue generated. Overseas imports trump overseas selling. Even the flags we wave on the Fourth of July are now made in China.

➤ Jobs are being outsourced to China and India at an alarming rate, with companies seeking cheaper ways of producing goods and services where the overhead is lower and the environment is more business-friendly.

➤ Obsolete industries are rapidly going out of business, leaving thousands of workers without jobs. And we're not creating enough new, sustainable industries to replace those that are becoming obsolete.

➤ Government needs a complete makeover. Currently it is too big, ineffective in some areas, and costs taxpayers too much. Take a look at major successful corporations, constantly tweaking, revamping, and streamlining operations to improve productivity and increase profits. Although government operates with a different goal, valuable lessons can be learned from for-profit corporations.

➤ The entrepreneurial spirit has weakened. Too many potential entrepreneurs lack the confidence to take businesses risks that would jump-start the economy.

➤ Small businesses need more decisive support at the grassroots level, including financial assistance through SBA-supported loan programs and an easier bureaucracy to navigate when it comes to doing business within a particular state.

➤ Two wars, in Iran and Afghanistan, have gobbled up billions with no income in return (but for a select few profiteers). Yes, defense spending is a crucial and necessary function of the federal government, but "Since 2001, military and security expenditures have soared by 119 percent."[2]

While these issues can seem overwhelming, there are long-term strategic plans that can be formed and implemented to move the economy to a more progressive track. However, the two immediate options for the government to stem the flow are to raise taxes—always a reliable comedy of bad PR for either the government or the hapless politician who suggests it—or to increase the deficit. The reality is that a tax increase actually *depletes* money from the economy. Sound ironic? It is. What we have been learning the hard way since 2009, is that consumer spending is what drives the economy and is, in itself, the only proven method of economic recovery; small business plays a vital role in facilitating it. Here's another look at how this plays out. One business writer has found that there are 18,311 big businesses in the US, and to reach zero unemployment each and every one of them would have to hire 655 new employees. But there are 27.5 million small businesses in the US, and if just half of them hired a single employee, unemployment would be at zero.[3] That simple math clearly proves my point in recognizing the vital role small business plays in the U.S. economy, and validates my premise in *One Hundred Pennies*.

A lot of people feel, understandably, that business taxes should be raised. But think again: this takes money that could be used to expand hiring. Tax breaks are a time-honored carrot to extend to businesses. A good example of withdrawing such a carrot was illustrated by a *New York Times* article on May14, 2011:

> *When Sears threatened last week to move its headquarters out of state, it should hardly have surprised Gov. Patrick K. Quinn, who in January dramatically raised income taxes. The tax increase made Illinois's total corporate tax burden heavier than all but 15 other states, according to the Tax Foundation, a non-profit research organization. That prompted other states to woo local companies.*[4]

And business owners see red when you tell them to pay more taxes. Their first impulse is to cut jobs. We are human, and for better or worse act on what we feel and think as much as on proven facts.

The alternative to raising taxes is the tried (and untrue) increase in deficit spending. Remember the 1980s? This method involves borrowing more money, increasing the menacing flashing numbers of the national deficit. While government can handle a higher debt load than private companies or individuals, there are limits. It may provide the illusion of being politically safer than higher taxes, but this is changing as people are beginning to realize that future generations of Americans will pay the price of our mistake.

When money behaves like a commodity, the federal government needs to borrow more, thereby reducing the amount available to lend to companies—where it might be used (remember?) to create jobs. Over the last few years, banks, reeling from the recession, overcompensated for their freewheeling sub-prime lending by pulling in their reins. Small businesses that previously relied on bank loans were hung out to dry. By the same token, excessive federal borrowing raises the cost of borrowing. There's a good reason for this: more federal money is then sacrificed for debt servicing, instead of being used for (potentially) valuable federal programs. Think about the Hoover Dam. These issues bode ill for the economic development and recovery from the Great Recession.

"GIVE ME MY MONEY'S WORTH"

Taxes, while never popular, are always necessary. Government is required to run our enormous country. But don't we want to see our tax dollars benefit us, rather than being frittered away on pork, or just plain being wasted due to incompetence? It is only human to prefer getting our money's worth, over pounding our fists in helpless outrage at the sense of being continuously ripped off. Enter the concept of earmarks—setting aside money in bigger appropriations bills for specific state projects (though a small portion of the federal budget). Earmarks tend to be high profile, publicity-generating machines, like the famous Gravina Island Bridge in Alaska, famously known as "the Bridge to Nowhere" and synonymous with pork. Hence earmarks' bad reputation as examples of wasteful spending.

FINDING A BALANCED ROLE FOR GOVERNMENT

The balanced role of government provides another important criterion for my argument. Instead of focusing on the role of reduced regulations in the current economic crisis, we need to explore the possibility of government's role in overregulation of businesses. Let's face it, people are not dependably self-regulating and never will be! Therefore markets, run by people, cannot be expected to offer 100 percent self-regulation in the best of times. Human nature will not permit it. No less than Alan Greenspan, chairman of the Federal Reserve Board, testified to Congress in 2008 that:

> As I wrote last March: those who have looked to the self-interest of lending institutions to protect shareholders' equity (myself especially) are in a state of shocked disbelief. Such counterparty surveillance is a central pillar of our financial markets' state of balance. If it fails, as occurred this year, market stability is undermined.[5]

As long ago as 1835, Alexis de Tocqueville noted in his work *Democracy in America* that the concept of enlightened self-interest provides a strong argument against the need for tight government regulation of business. Consider that this was a full decade before the concept of Communism was first expressed by Karl Marx and Friedrich Engels, itself an idea which has been played out over the course of the post-World War I twentieth century and died a natural death. Indeed, does Communism not provide the most dramatic argument against excessive regulation?

Tocqueville wrote, "The Americans… are fond of explaining almost all the actions of their lives by the principle of interest rightly understood; they show with complacency *how an enlightened regard for themselves constantly prompts them to assist each other, and inclines them willingly to sacrifice a portion of their time and property to the welfare of the state.*"[6]

But bear in mind that even such a brilliant mind as Tocqueville's allowed for different circumstances. And we live in a far different world from that of 1835, when a still-developing, pre-Civil War America consisted of only twenty-four states, and slavery accounted for a significant share of economic growth. As was true then, however, government's role continues to be to spot changes effectively and not be caught short when change, however subtle, occurs.

REGULATION AND/OR INNOVATION

Government's real job in terms of the economy is to accommodate businesses and make it easy for them to flourish and prosper. To enable this, government has to exercise some controls over the economy—clearly thought-out, monitored, and minimal—to achieve its goals in terms of thriving small businesses. The anarchy at the opposite end of the proposition—no regulations—is as fatal to free enterprise and economic development as its reverse, the totalitarian state control exemplified by Communism.

China, a rare example of a successful Communist state, achieves that success not by adhering to the socialist path, but by effectively declaring a capitalist economy to be in keeping with socialism. However, as Chinese billionaires increase in number (something inconceivable under Mao!), it is easy to see that the introduction of "state capitalism" has resulted in businesses structured like private-sector companies, though the government maintains controlling interests. Some experts say that, for all the good it has done for the Chinese economy, it is not without inherent faults and limits, especially in terms of promoting innovation.[7] Also, by some estimates it is actually becoming harder for a private-sector company to do business in

China.[8] And as far as efficient regulation goes, just think of the lethal pet-food and milk disasters of recent years.

Innovation, credited by many—including me—as the primary way for any country to maintain strong competitiveness in the world economy, holds freedom of thought as being implicit. While China has enjoyed remarkable economic growth (in the economic sector at least), since shedding the strict doctrinaire Communism of forty years ago, it is still a prime example of the need for careful balance as far as government fulfilling its proper role in a national economy.

READJUSTING GOVERNMENT'S FOCUS

It can be argued that the best function of government—beyond such basics as defense, foreign policy, domestic security, social services, and a few others—is decidedly *not* to do everything. At the same time, it cannot stand idly by and let the chips fall where they may, market-wise. Rather, government's responsibility is to see that things get done, while at the same time ensuring that big business behaves itself—specifically that it does not swagger arrogantly over small-business, consumers, or the environment, let alone the public interest, in order to achieve profit. Thus defining the role of government at all levels is the continuing struggle that faces us as a nation.

We need to adjust the focus of governmental efforts to find a new balance in a post-recession economy. The global economy is rapidly changing, and government's long- and short-term strategic plans have to change as well, in order for our country to remain globally competitive. For example, excessive spending is a bad policy, especially during an economic downturn. The government trying to create jobs is similar to saying we're going to increase your taxes or increase the deficit to justify hiring new employees. The private sector creates jobs, not the government.

My own contention is that the best place to get the most out of each government dollar spent, is in the realm of supporting small businesses and invention. Ironically, this does not require huge tax dollars; in fact quite on the contrary, as will be discussed later in the book. Simple ideas—such as supplying centralized business information for current and potential entrepreneurs, providing viable support for SBA-backed loans, etc.—will not only provide useful, easily accessible information and resources for businesses, but empower individuals to take the risk of starting or expanding a business. As a valuable side effect, we will see a reduction in political and policy attention to the general role of government, and business as usual. We will see a government that actually (hold on to your hat) *does* something for small business.

As it stands now, looked at from this perspective, the Small Business Administration's methods are obsolete in today's economy. Sound like an overstatement? Not at all, especially when established small businesses that go to the SBA for help are often turned away without meaningful assistance, or when banks that are supposed to provide SBA-backed loan requests either refuse to lend or demand a litter of documents that makes the process time-consuming and often unmanageable for most small-business owners. This example will illustrate my point:

John owns a printing company and has been in business for over thirty-two years. He had a staff of forty-three but recently had to downsize because printing is quickly becoming an obsolete industry, as most of his customers can now print documents, business cards, flyers, brochures, etc. from the comfort of their offices, as both software and hardware are accessible at affordable prices. However, John developed a concept that would allow his customers to utilize his services online with a more efficient product than the do-it-yourself printing concept. But, he needed a $200,000 *loan to integrate this idea into his current business model, so he went to his local bank, which provided SBA-backed loans. He went through the process of applying for a loan only to be turned down; he was considered to be a high-risk customer because he was being innovative and reinventing his business; in addition, his previous year's taxes reflected a loss which was due to the economic recession. The SBA may have sponsored fifty percent if John took out a second mortgage on the collateral in his home. Mind you, he had maintained a checking and savings account with this bank for the past thirty years, with a total monthly checking account average of $80,000 over the past five years.*

So the question is, where is the support for small business owners like John?

RESTORING ECONOMIC UNIQUENESS THROUGH REINVENTION

The economic uniqueness of the U.S. will be restored in the same manner in which it was originated: by being fearless about developing new and better ways of doing things, about creating new products and jobs that are homegrown rather than imported, and about supporting and encouraging goods and services made in America. One promising area is that of reinvention, of finding new ways of doing old things.

The Founding Fathers themselves were nothing if not Enlightenment-inspired self-starters who thought far outside the box. We need now to recreate this same level of excitement and invention (albeit adjusted for modern tastes and needs) to jump-start something the Founders did not envision: a floundering U.S. economy *and* a rapidly evolving global economy. Even amid today's trials and tribulations, it is worth a backward glance in the Founders' direction, if only to recapture this vital ingredient that fell away from our former economic self-determination. Having rescued the country from British domination, the Founders set up shop and did business in new ways, formulating practical solutions to whatever problems arose, free of Colonial edicts.

Think about these words describing a young Benjamin Franklin: "He put aside speculations on the nature of reality in favor of living as a reasonable creature in contact with the world that presented itself though the evidence of his senses."[9] Now imagine the reaction of the man who co-authored the Declaration of Independence and the Constitution, to the notion of sub-prime lending or junk bonds, or outsourcing thousands of jobs to foreign countries.

Franklin and the early Founders did not formulate ideas out of thin air; everything related to real conditions in real time. These were people who accepted reality and behaved accordingly. And they did not stop there. Improvement and expansion, rather than built-in obsolescence, were understood as prime components of their vision. There is a reason that the Constitution is as relevant today as it was in 1776! An inherent trust in the "spirit of a people who had endured and who felt that much that was promising lay ahead"[10] informed its substance, and a committed revival of this same spirit is inherent in the restoration of economic uniqueness.

SOCIAL ISSUES PLACE SECOND

Our political landscape runs the spectrum of conservative to liberal and everything in between, but the two main topics in question are always fiscal policy and social issues. Understandably we need to have jobs in order to buy groceries and take care of our families. So shouldn't fiscal policy trump social issues, especially during difficult times like the Great Recession? What about the environment? Some people feel it's best to address the needs of the most unfortunate first, then to police morality, putting economic factors at the end. While I don't mean to be cruel or insensitive, it's the wrong order. Americans know the importance of social issues, so the creation of a strong new economy (and a protected society) requires that such issues take a back seat to true quality-of-life concerns:

- ➤ Jobs.
- ➤ A strong economy.
- ➤ Domestic and international security.

Am I preaching a heartless libertarianism here? Not at all. It's just that a strong economy creates jobs, fueling the economic engine to support social progress and uplift those who are in need.

THE KEY ELEMENT: THE ENTREPRENEURIAL SPIRIT

Instead of CEOs in private jets, how about focusing on leaders of small businesses? They are the people who will definitively help to restore our own economic leadership by strengthening our economy now and in the future. Small business is the specific arena for advances—both technical and economic—that provide job-creation rather than job-exportation; but intervention is required. We have lost our way in the past few years, getting caught up in the scandal of corporate greed and falling markets, and forgetting that the true entrepreneur is struggling to find his/her way through the chaos. What must be done? We must put our country back on track by setting our priorities in order. Let us restore the entrepreneurial spirit in America today.

Restoring that spirit is not just about creating a new business model, recognizing that the idea is good, and then setting it into action. The true entrepreneurial spirit exists in the belief-system of the end user. As Proverbs 23 has it, "As a man thinks, so he is." If you believe in your belly that you can do it, then you can. And if you had to name but one thing that made the U.S. not only great, but possible, you would have to identify it as this same belief in our capabilities. Covered wagons would never have crossed the prairies and mountains without it. Skill alone is not enough; neither is strength. While part of this book contains suggestions for re-cultivating the skills to restore the economy, that part will always be eclipsed by that tried-and-true yet magical element: the uniquely American *can-do* spirit…the same spirit that, as some of our "Greatest Generation" grand-parents put it, won the Second World War.

IN SUMMARY
Our current problems in a nutshell:

- ➤ The world economy is rapidly changing, which affects the U.S. economy.
- ➤ Technological advances are making it easier to eliminate workers as some industries become obsolete.
- ➤ We are falling behind as the world power in development of more efficient technologies and services.
- ➤ We are importing more than we are exporting. This is true even without considering energy.
- ➤ The entrepreneurial spirit has weakened. Too many potential entrepreneurs lack the confidence to take business risks that would jump-start the economy.
- ➤ Through outsourcing, we are losing jobs and industries from the private sector to foreign countries in a constant search for cheaper overhead and production costs.
- ➤ Banks are extremely unwilling to lend to small businesses.
- ➤ Worker talent is wasted when many who collect unemployment are not driven to seek new work until their current benefits expire.
- ➤ Small business needs more decisive support at the grassroots level.

2

SPOTTING THE PROBLEMS

How many times have you heard the phrase, "too big to fail"? Probably more than you can count. If we are to believe its premise—that corporate failure is the economic equivalent to an atom bomb (as well it can be)—we must also be willing to look at the other side of the equation. What happens when thousands of small businesses are allowed to fail? I believe that the key reason for the prolonged Great Recession is the failure of thousands of small businesses and the stagnated growth of those that have survived.

With companies like GM and Ford hovering on the brink, a dramatic rescue was played out for the world to see. Only in that sector has significant action been taking to put out the fire and permit those companies to get back on their feet again (which, to their credit, they have). Their failure would certainly have reverberated painfully throughout the world, far beyond their employees and stockholders, as we saw with the notorious Enron disaster of 2001. The message we all took home was that if huge corporations fail, we not only suffer terrible consequences in terms of job and revenue loss, but lose the only economic engine we have to stave off future catastrophe. This is accurate, but only partially so. And we were already warned.

The economist Joseph Stiglitz, one-time chief economist at the World Bank, foretold as much when he said, back in 1995, "When enterprises become too big, and interconnections too tight, there is a risk that the quality of economic decisions deteriorate, and the 'too big to fail' problem rears its ugly head."[11] Stiglitz was not crying wolf in the midst of Clinton-era prosperity. From the standpoint of 2003, when his book was published, Enron had already occurred to prove his point. His prediction was all too true.

After Stiglitz's warning, the next big tremor arrived in 1999, when the federal government sought to repeal the Glass-Steagall Act of the Great Depression. This New Deal law split up commercial and investment banking "as a way of preventing ordinary banks from becoming part of the Wall Street underwriting and trading culture."[12] And Glass-Steagall *was* repealed that same year, by a heavily partisan vote. The barn door was now open, with some big horses ready to make a run for it.

One of the few congressional voices in the wilderness was Congressman John D. Dingell, Jr. of Michigan. His father, John D. Dingell, Sr., who had also served in Congress for twenty-two years, had helped write the original act. It is worth quoting John Dingell when, speaking on the House floor, he warned that:

> *What we are creating now is a group of institutions which are too big to fail...under this legislation, the whole of the regulatory structure is so obfuscated and so confused that liability in one area is going to fall over into liability in the next. Taxpayers are going to be called upon to cure the failures we are creating tonight, and it is going to cost a lot of money, and it is coming.*[13]

Sound like an uncannily accurate prediction? It was. There's nothing like 20-20 hindsight to provide a lens through which we can now see what followed: the September 2008 collapse of Lehman Brothers, credited with touching off the major phase of the Great Recession. Ten days later, with the insurance giant AIG foundering, the Bush administration and the Federal Reserve Board proposed what would become the "most substantial government intervention in the financial market since the Great Depression." According to the *Wall Street Journal*, in one private meeting, Secretary of the Treasury Henry Paulson told lawmakers, "If it doesn't pass, then heaven help us all." [14]

Considering what happened to the economy with the bailout, one shudders to think of the alternative. The first federal bailout bill almost did not pass, after being voted down in the House of Representatives. The very next day, the Dow Jones dropped just under 1,000 points and the bill passed on its second attempt. But with the deficit running at an all-time high, can the government continue with such massive bailouts?

To give the devil his due, it is possible that the repeal of Glass-Steagall might have aided, peripherally, in the eventual recovery; or at least, weakened its steep decline. The repeal did succeed in enabling companies to enlarge the margin by which they could purchase other companies beyond the confines of their specific industries. Bank of America, for example, was able to buy the investment firm of Merrill Lynch, coming to the rescue of (some) jobs and investment resources. But does this justify the repeal?

Many experts say no, and argue that such benefits are irrelevant. It is hardly coincidence that the deregulatory zeal symbolized by repeal of Glass-Steagall appeared at the same time that the sub-prime derivative market intensified.[15] The best, if simplistic, explanation for the latter describes them as stocks and bonds sold to people who could not afford them— people who were ultimately destined to default. And when these unqualified mortgage-holders began to do so, the cracks in the foundation of the sub-prime mortgages gave way, collapsing the building of derivatives with it.

True to Congressman Dingell's prediction, this catastrophic breakdown in the real-estate market—within a severely impaired post-Glass-Steagall-repeal regulatory environment—pulled down not just the American economy, but that of the entire world. Consider this: better (rather than more), well-implemented government regulation would not have stifled the honest growth of even big business.

As you can see, the focus here remains on regulatory/deregulatory effects upon big business. My theory, shared by many experts, maintains that the focus on big business caused many errors, and furthermore, that the big-business focus itself was misbegotten. While big business was never the largest generator of jobs, its expertise at destroying jobs (as seen in 2008 and 2009), both directly and indirectly, shook the economy to its core. As big businesses often provide a market for small businesses, that market, in response, declined.

As history proves, when the government seeks to ease up on the big players, it is the smaller fish in the pond that suffer. And this provides the entrée for my theory.

THERE IS A CLEAR action plan that can be implemented, one that would both rev up the economy *and* prevent future market cataclysms. The information is out there. Even in the worst economy, some small businesses not only survive, but thrive. Unfortunately, the majority do not.

A good example on the plus side is that of Chicago's Kim and Scott Holstein. A bit of their story follows:

> *What began as a side project in their home kitchen has blossomed into Kim & Scott's Gourmet Pretzels, a $10 million, 80-employee company that specializes in classic soft pretzels but also includes stuffed varieties like "Pizza Pretzel" and "Grilled Cheese" that double as meals. The couple initially sold to local bakeries and cafes in Chicago, but now find their Bavarian treats on the shelves of Whole Foods, Super Target, Walmart and other major grocery chains across the*

country. Scott, 43, is the Chief Operating Officer, while Kim, 44, calls herself Chief Inspiration Officer. Like many great businesses, Kim & Scott's began with day-job frustrations. They met in a bookstore, fell in love, married, and had three kids. And in the process of raising a family, they raised a very successful business.

As Kim Holstein says, "One…challenge for a small business [is] to not only get on the shelf in the frozen aisle, but to stay there. It's a very competitive marketplace, often owned by the big companies. They have the funds for slotting fees so they can buy and hold their space. It makes it very difficult for the little guys to succeed. However, we have been making our way, and being a WBE [Women's Business Enterprise] certified business has helped us tremendously with reducing the slotting dollars or eliminating the dollars usually needed."[16]

Are most successful small business owners Harvard or Wharton graduates with glamorous pedigrees? Hardly. They are average Americans with specific dreams (rather than vague fantasies) and the tenacity to see them through—along with the ability to ask questions and get answers as needed. The overall payoff from their success their continuous and firm contribution to national economic growth and development. *Sure* development that can withstand disruption from other sectors of the economy.

THE TERRIBLE IRONY is that small businesses are too often overlooked (i.e., permitted to fail) by government, and/or crushed by big business. It is too easy for those in power to forget that one hundred pennies make a dollar, and that one hundred million pennies make one million dollars. It's fine for them to see the trillions of dollars exemplified in the gross national product, but not to be blind to the small amounts that when combined make up the big numbers. After all, the majority of those small

amounts—those pennies—is determined by small businesses'
contribution. Remember? Out of every dollar received in our
nation's GDP, sixty cents comes from small businesses, and this
money is retained and re-circulated by the community. Contrast
this with the following statistics:

1. 6 cents of every dollar spent with a Big Box retailer
   is retained/ re-circulated in a community.
   (Source: Rocky Mountain Institute)
2. 20 cents of every dollar spent with a chain store
   is retained/ re-circulated in a community.
   (Source: Small Business Administration)

So why are small businesses always the last to receive necessary assistance? Too often they are the first casualties of a
downturn. From there, watch the unemployment numbers rise
as the economy stagnates and growth is significantly slowed.
With small businesses representing such a major force in the
economy, proactively addressing their needs with a governmental response to small-business solutions will avert further
catastrophe, especially in challenging economic times.

Small businesses are virtually never the catalysts for economic
crises. These crises are most often the result of poorly made decisions
by large corporations, of government undersight, and of failure to
notice the signs (or take subsequent action) of trouble brewing.

The government made the only decision possible in late 2008
when, swallowing its massive pride, it reached for taxpayer dollars in the form of TARP. As Lehman Brothers illustrated, some
corporations really *are* too big to fail. TARP bailouts were given
to the high-flying big boys who had made bad choices, driven
by greed rather than common sense. Ironically, the federal government may break even or make a profit on at least a few of
the TARP-saved companies. The TARP process included government purchase of stock. Selling such a stock a year later produced
some pleasant surprises, most notably with General Motors.

But there were no TARP bailouts for small companies. Wall Street prevailed over Main Street and small companies had to fend for themselves—at a significant cost to both the economy and to jobs. Banks held onto the money they had been given to lend, with year-end executive bonuses that were scandalously lavish. "Don't ask, don't tell," in the useless parlance for gays in the military, seemed to be the new slogan for banks.

Many small business owners, as well as everyday citizens, were left feeling bitterly disenfranchised. Who could blame us? TARP bailouts likely extended the recession, slowing its recovery. As a result, Democrats suffered in the November 2010 elections, taking what President Obama memorably called a "shellacking."

Whatever the various arguments, the varying abuses, and the genuine needs, were TARP and its related measures necessary? Were they truly a good idea? I think the answer is yes. TARP prevented further damage to a shaky national and world economy. Without it, hundreds of thousands of additional jobs may have been lost. A few more of the giants would have failed and our banking system itself would have taken a slide—a disturbing notion to the majority of us who save our money in banks rather than under the mattress.

Democratic free enterprise is set up to ensure an even playing field, not equal results. While there is no ceiling to achievement, there is no floor protecting one from failure. However, since the big corporate collapses of 2009, these theories were rendered unaffordable, and TARP was formulated. In short, the bank versus the mattress.

And this is where our problem lies. How does government serve the people effectively on all levels of the playing field? And how does government understand that a focus on the most visible 40 pennies that make up a dollar is bad strategy? The remaining 60 pennies represented by small business suffer or fall short. What we have with a 40-penny focus is government micromanagement that crushes initiative under the illusory banner of preventing misbehavior.

IN SUMMARY

The key to successful government is not micromanagement, but serving the needs of citizens by:

- ➤ Providing assistance.
- ➤ Creating opportunities for economic growth and development.
- ➤ Establishing safeguards for the interests of its people.
- ➤ Securing the standards by which we live.
- ➤ Providing protection from foreign and domestic threats.

The key to successful business is to:

- ➤ Invent and create sustainable products/services.
- ➤ Stimulate the economic engine, encouraging commerce and trade.
- ➤ Enable opportunity to flourish and prosper beyond government walls.
- ➤ Create jobs.
- ➤ Be socially responsible.
- ➤ Help generate revenue in order to allow the government and public services to function.

Remember, without successful business we cannot have a government, and without a government we cannot have a stable society. Both of these binaries need to work together, each bringing its distinctive strengths to the blend. Trouble arises when business and government engage in a love-hate relationship, producing a tug-of-war rather than the productive teamwork of, say, a Kim & Scott's Gourmet Pretzels.

From a spiritual perspective, the negative energy wasted in tug-of-war struggles dramatically slows progress: the progress of business, of government, of society, and of the nation.

3

THE GREAT RECESSION

B y now, the zeitgeist of *One Hundred Pennies* becomes clear and emerges into a fuller picture. Some problems will be solved; even Great Recessions eventually end. Unfortunately, the current situation remains serious despite the light at the end of the tunnel. Outward details change, but the underlying situation—where my strategies are directed—remains all too often the same.

Think about what happened on December 16, 2010, for example. Don't remember? That was the day the New York State Department of Labor reported the addition of 700 private-sector jobs in November. Okay, so here's how things stood at that moment in time:

> New York State unemployment 8.3%
> New York City unemployment 9.1%
> National unemployment 9.8%

"Like the nation as a whole," the press release commented, "New York State's economic recovery from this recession has been very uneven to date."[17] No joke was intended. New York City's rates in anything are high, given its status as one of the world's largest cities.

You can safely bet that at least one in seven New Yorkers was either un- or underemployed at any given time during the recession. The unemployment rate is blind to such nuances, measuring only the number of people actively job seeking. Those who've given up, or whose unemployment benefits have terminated, don't figure into the statistic.

At the same time, according to the government at year's end, national unemployment statistics changed little in 2010, holding steady around that 9.8 percent number. As with New York City, bear in mind those who dropped out of the race altogether and remain uncounted.

The civilian labor force participation rate held at 64.5 percent in November, and the employment population ratio was essentially unchanged at 58.2 percent. The number of persons employed part-time for economic reasons (sometimes referred to as involuntary part-time workers) was little changed over the month, at 9 million. These individuals were working part-time because their hours had been cut back, or because they were unable to find full-time jobs.

About 2.5 million persons were marginally attached to the labor force in November, up from 2.3 million a year earlier. (The data are not seasonally adjusted.) These individuals were not in the labor force, wanted and were available for work, and had looked for a job sometime in the prior twelve months. They were not counted as employed because they had not searched for work in the four weeks preceding the survey.

Among the marginally attached, there were 1.3 million discouraged workers in November, an increase of 421,000 from a year earlier. Discouraged workers are persons not currently looking for work because they believe that no jobs are available for them. The remaining 1.2 million persons marginally attached to the labor force had not searched for work in the four weeks preceding the survey for reasons such as school attendance or family responsibilities. What is the bottom line for unemployment statistics? We need to double or triple the numbers to account for those, as noted above, who have either left the system or taken less advantageous jobs, and are paid off the books, so to speak.

Awaiting the end of unemployment benefits is the rule for some jobseekers; only then do they begin an active search, a move I've seen within my industry and don't recommend. It's better to accept a temporary position paying a bit less in order to keep skills sharp, than to wait for unemployment benefits to expire. What happens? Two years have gone by and your skills are no longer current. You have become less desirable to an employer. Think of it this way: would you permit a doctor to treat you who hadn't been practicing medicine for the past two years? This is an employer's perspective on such a huge résumé gap. Therefore, prolonging unemployment benefits can prove detrimental to a person rendered complacent by collecting benefits rather than proactively seeking employment.

This not only adds to numbers, but darkens public perceptions of the unemployed in general. Then you have calls for system reform—especially in terms of the desperately unemployed, who have no idea of how to survive once benefits expire.

What about across the pond? We often hear of lavish governmental benefits in Great Britain, where many enjoy living on the dole. But the situation in Britain is only somewhat better. While the December 2010 unemployment rate was reported as 7.9 percent, a second statistic (put out at the same time) indicated a *working age unemployment rate* of 70.1 percent.[18] This would seem to calculate the missing factors in the American figures and, as such, is to be regarded soberly. Take another look at the American unemployment statistics with "70.1 percent" in mind.

THE MONSTER: CAUSE AND EFFECT

"Monster" is not too strong a word to describe the Great Recession. It is a monster in several ways; with a worldwide economy that took a hit of a volume unknown since the 1930s, don't even think of the horrifying might-have-beens and almost-weres. What's in front of us is alarming enough. The challenge for us is to *minimize the length of this recession* so that we can get back on a fast track to economic growth.

Derivatives (such as bonds based on sub-prime mortgages) have figured prominently in examinations of the current crisis. They originated back in the 1800s as a method to protect farmers' financial stability. Sensible practices, formulated to safeguard hardworking farmers' finances, eventually degenerated into a quick shot at easy money. While there are exceptions to every rule, the rule carries the day in terms of general behavior. Many workers in the financial industry have one goal: to make as much money as possible. Cheating may not figure into their equation, but that is what generally happens with such a simplistic goal that desires only to be met, nothing else.

Again and again, television news has shown us perp-walk after executive perp-walk, and we wonder aloud—don't these people ever learn? What we forget is human nature, and that excessive profits blind people to the moral implications of their actions. They are further blind to practical dangers (think of Martha Stewart and her self-condemning emails!). By far the most serious danger is attracting government investigation. That is usually when the walls of Jericho come down, the scheme collapses, and handcuffs are fitted around Hermes cuff links.

The sub-prime market, even without predatory lending, risked collapse if the real-estate bubble burst, and as we now know this is exactly what occurred. And sufficient unto the day would have been its problems, without the increased complexity of derivatives. Ultimately, the vast, short-term profits born of such maneuvering deflected attention from more important issues…from the fact that lasting economic growth comes from innovation, from invention, and new solutions, not from quick-profit growth more akin to a pyramid scheme than sound financial practice. Indeed, think of April 2010 and the foul mess that petroleum giant BP created for itself in the Gulf of Mexico. Though not a finance company, BP's oil-spill catastrophe serves as an apt metaphor for corporate meltdowns of all kinds. The root problems are identical.

In keeping with the same kind of Armageddon metaphor exemplified by BP, a look at the infamous "trickle down" economics is better seen as deluge economics, with little salvaged from the flood. When the dam bursts, small businesses are the first casualties. When the dam springs a leak (regardless of who's at fault), repairs must be paid for. The best solution is to keep the dam from breaking at all. And this is so important: shore up the dam through appropriate controls, *but don't clog it up*! That way, the small business downstream is protected.

The downside to small businesses' flexibility is that, in terms of hiring, they are not so deeply entrenched as their big business counterparts. Thus they may lay off more quickly and consequently go down more quickly. Such a fluid workforce, as we have seen, falls outside of government bailout protection and is left to fend for itself. For an easy example, let's put aside the recession and just think of the myriad small businesses in the Gulf of Mexico left devastated by giant BP's oil spill.

All urgent problems, no? In that government had swung too far toward deregulation, they are fundamental. But they also reveal more: a fundamental obstacle in our approach to the economy. While pre-2008 corporate America was engaged in the financial equivalent of a Bacchanalian orgy, the small businesspeople were starving. Yes, the necessity of saving large corporations was clear, but so was something else: equivalent public resentment at Wall Street-style big business. Hence, the Occupy Wall Street movement was formed. Although lacking a cohesive message, it was evident that people were trying to speak out with one voice about big-business corruption and the impact on society as a whole. As you've guessed by now, I do not see large corporations themselves as being the main problem with the economy nor are they the "enemy." Neither do I see correcting them as the *sine qua non* solution to recessionary woes.

MERGERS AND acquisitions by large corporations are another area affected in this economy. As companies seek economies of scale, this leads to further loss of back-office support positions. Today, when two large companies merge, the support staff for one company (using advancing technology) can handle support functions for *both* companies. Pink slips then litter the ground. Not only that, but even more jobs stand to be lost as the new company realizes that some support functions can be handled from outside the United States. Here it is again, that word: *outsourcing*. We'll be discussing it at greater length in the next chapter.

Companies are of course keen to find cheaper and more efficient methods of providing the same or better services. Any quality loss (ever spend twenty minutes with the Bangalore call center over a five-minute matter?) from offshore outsourcing is, in conventional wisdom, far eclipsed by decreased costs and increased profits. In some cases, such as customer service for electronics, the loss is in quality (as with the overlong Bangalore phone conversation) rather than product. "Word of mouth" advertising has taken on a whole new meaning as well, when all I have to do is go online, Google the name of the product, and click on "Reviews." Thousands of customers' feedback is available in an instant.

The way out of the Great Recession is not for government to create more jobs, but for government to empower the private sector to create more jobs by providing incentives, reorganizing itself, encouraging businesses to stay here in the US, support US-made products, and create a resurgence of "Made in the USA" pride that will reverberate in every home across the nation. The argument I hear all the time is that products made oversees are cheaper than those made here in the US. Although the argument has some validity, it is not always the case. But even if it were so, how patriotic is it to know that by spending a few extra dollars you're actually saving jobs here and supporting businesses that refuse to outsource? What will drive people to look deliberately at labels, not just for the designer name but for the country of manufacture? Only a keen awareness of the importance to the health of our economy that supporting goods and services made in the U.S. has on the overall lives of Americans.

When businesses realize that consumers are driven not only by designer labels on a product but by their country of manufacture, it ultimately encourages businesses to bring back their overseas operations and hire Americans to manufacture goods and provide services on American soil. For this to work, government has to provide the right environment for businesses, and to have joint discussions that would bring about a mutually beneficial solution across the board. However, our world will not be the same; rising global competition and rapidly evolving technology will see to that. We have to be better than ever, a leaner and more efficient economic power led by a proactive government that uses common sense and good judgment to move ideas forward, while encouraging invention and small-business growth, thereby fueling new, sustainable-job-creating companies.

4

LONG-TERM PROBLEMS
The Real Nature of the Economy

Doesn't it often seem that just when things are improving, some new statistic is released which shows the opposite? At the beginning of 2011, both the housing market and unemployment rates remained in the doldrums. We could take some consolation from the fact that things were not getting worse, though not much.

Over the past few decades, our economy has digressed from being one intent on doing things proactively, to one occupied with first paying for things, and then…? Just taking the money. We see where it's gotten us. The illusion that we were getting richer as a society ran strong, at least through 2007. Perhaps we were, but at the same time the divide between higher and lower income levels expanded. And, though we are still by far the largest economy worldwide, we are slowly falling into a less-than-dominant one.

As you've noticed by now, there is no shortage of irony in this analysis. Here's yet another example: we became a greater import economy, even to the extent of importing money to help resolve our debt problems. Time for a more penetrating look at what kind of society we have become, of what kind we should be.

So what is the key to both economic reform *and* advancement? Dealing with things exactly as they are. Six major factors affect our current economy:

➤ The trade-balance deficit.

➤ Outsourcing of industries and jobs.

➤ Obsolete industries, as human capital is replaced by technology without creating enough sustainable jobs to take us into the future.

➤ High taxes in some key states like New York.

➤ Overregulation of business.

➤ Lack of effective government incentives for a healthy business climate.

TRADE-BALANCE DEFICIT

The federal government, the Department of Commerce, the Census Bureau, and the Bureau of Economic Analysis all release monthly figures on the trade balance. The summary for the latest results as of this writing (dated November 2010 but released January 13, 2011),[19] states:

> *The U.S. Census Bureau and the U.S. Bureau of Economic Analysis, through the Department of Commerce, announced today that total November exports of **$159.6 billion** and imports of **$198.0 billion** resulted in a goods and services deficit of **$38.3** billion, down from $38.4 billion in October, revised. November exports were $1.2 billion more than October exports of $158.4 billion. November imports were $1.1 billion more than October imports of $196.8 billion.*
>
> *In November, the goods deficit increased to $0.1 billion from October to $51.2 billion, and the services surplus increased $0.2 billion to $12.9 billion. Exports of goods increased $1.3 billion to $113.5 billion, and imports of goods increased $1.4 billion to $164.7 billion. Exports of services decreased $0.1 billion to $46.2 billion, and the imports of services decreased $0.3 billion to $33.3 billion.*

The goods and services deficit increased $3.0 billion from November 2009 to November 2010. Exports were up $20.7 billion, or 14.9 percent, and imports were up $23.7 billion, or 13.6 percent.

OUTSOURCING

The topic of outsourcing jobs has become a hot-button issue of debate in the presidential campaign of 2012, but guess what? This has been an ongoing trend for over a decade. Forrester Research predicts that by 2015 we would have lost more than 3.5 million jobs overseas.

The pressure of competition in an ever-growing global market forces large companies to offer customers more for less, thereby reducing a company's profit margin. In order to remain competitive and maximize profits, company executives are forced to reduce the overhead costs on the expense portion of the profit-and-loss report. One of the highest costs in overhead is human capital. Ironically, it is also one of a company's greatest assets. But shifting the pendulum of talent from one region within the U.S. to another part of the world has been an effective way to reduce that expense. The name for this, as we've come to know well, is outsourcing.

Though technically defined as hiring another company to do a specific job, the term has come to mean relocating support positions overseas, facilitated by increasingly effective communications technology. Enter the era of "Kevin," that anonymous call-center operator who attempts to answer your questions about anything from a local checking account to changing your Internet provider.

Sending support jobs to Bangalore, India, yields technologically expert workers whose salaries are but a fraction of their American counterparts in identical jobs. With an 11.5 hour time difference, the call center in India commences work just a few hours later. The Indian center has the work done, with little or no overtime, before the New York-based firm has even arrived at their office the next day. The Indian subcontractors are overjoyed at the increases in their pay, with the added benefit of not having to leave home. Sound ideal? It is. And not just for them—the American firm saves thousands and improves the bottom line for their shareholders. Everyone is happy, except for the laid-off American workers whose jobs evaporated in the wake of outsourcing.

I had the chance to see this in operation. A branch of my firm is located in Tampa, Florida, where telecommunications and telephone customer-service support were once abundant. But the party has ended. Many of these jobs have now been exported to other offshore locations where the cost of labor (and of living) is far lower in comparison to the United States. Consider also that many of these jobs, including manufacturing, originally chose the American south for their factories to avoid northern unions and higher labor costs!

Need more proof? A recent report from the AFL-CIO aptly summarizes the serious dilemma of outsourcing, and its consequences to U.S. industry:

> *Since 2001, the nation has lost more than 2.5 million manufacturing jobs and more than 850,000 professional service and information sector jobs. No one knows for sure how many of these jobs have been lost due to increased import competition and shifts in production abroad, since no comprehensive official data are collected. Various independent estimates indicate the number of white-collar jobs lost to shipping work overseas over the past few years is in the hundreds of thousands, and millions are at risk in the next five to ten years. But the number of jobs lost need not be overwhelming in order to concern policymakers: increased*

overseas outsourcing also undermines wages and working conditions in those jobs left behind and threatens the long-term health of the economy.[20]

Additionally, the AFL-CIO report supplied some equally grim statistics:

➤ 3 million-plus manufacturing jobs have vanished since 1998. Estimates are that 59 percent have been lost due to the manufacturing trade deficit.
➤ 400,000 to 600,000 professional and information service jobs have moved overseas in roughly the same period.
➤ One-third of all major financial firms are sending work overseas, with surveys showing that this is likely to double in the next two years.
➤ Information technology jobs are particularly hard hit, including the creation of software. This work can easily be done away from American corporate headquarters.
➤ State governments are outsourcing "back-office" jobs. Forty states, at least, contract food-stamp benefit cards work overseas (perhaps increasing the need for food stamps stateside?).
➤ Projections of jobs to be moved overseas by 2015 range from 3.5 million to 14 million.

The AFL-CIO also reports that new jobs will tend to pay less and provide fewer worker benefits. The report concluded with a dark outlook for the future of the American economy as a whole. "Trade-related job loss," it states, "does not just hurt individual workers and their families. Entire communities are affected negatively as tax revenues fall, dependency on public assistance increases, and incomes stagnate." Furthermore, "and as the offshoring and job loss spread to sectors with high technology and skills that drive innovation and productivity, it puts the long-term competitiveness of the American economy at risk."[21] No quick recovery for the job market can be found there, can it?

Should you wonder if labor unions are to blame (and a lot of people believe they are), prepare to be disabused of this notion. The same sorry conclusions were confirmed by a December 2010 study by business research organization, The Hackett Group. This study concluded, in part, that:

> *There's no end in sight for the jobless recovery in business functions such as corporate finance and IT, in large part due to the accelerated movement of work to India and other offshore locations....The dramatic job losses seen by the U.S. and European companies in 2008 and 2009 are expected to continue through 2014.*

> ➤ *The Hackett Group's latest research found that close to 1.1 million jobs in corporate finance, IT, and other business functions were lost at large U.S. and European companies due to a combination of offshoring, productivity improvements, and lack of economic growth. Over 1.3 million additional jobs will disappear by 2014, with offshoring becoming a larger and larger factor each year. These figures represent annual job loss rates of close to twice those seen from 2000 to 2007....*
> ➤ *According to Honorio Padron, global business services practice leader for The Hackett Group, "A number of factors have helped create this situation. Certainly, the savings that can be generated by moving jobs to low-cost labor markets is too great for most companies to ignore. In addition, many companies have become much more mature in their use of offshore resources. They began with shared service centers nearly a decade ago, taking basic transactional areas offshore on a one-off basis. But today*

we're seeing the rapid ascendance of comprehensive cross-functional Global Business Services operations that are moving far beyond transactional work, to handle the lion's share of the support function for many companies. The result is a globalization trend from which there's simply no turning back.

The die is cast. A trend from which there's "no turning back" —there you have it. Is the quality of work done by these off-shore workers perfect? No. But despite some dissatisfaction, the growth of outsourcing increases. A 2010 poll in the United Kingdom showed that certain dissatisfaction runs high. There, at least three-quarters of businesses have expressed disappointment with the quality results of offshoring. So why are jobs not being brought back to the country of origin if the quality of service in jeopardy? The business leaders, undeterred, intend to keep up and even expand offshore outsourcing. And, incredibly, this is despite 94 percent feeling that a focus on cost rather than quality would increase the chance of projects failing.[22]

These are some very curious figures, are they not? I would like to know more. Why are businesses deciding to focus on costs with what is clearly a noticeable risk to quality? Is a slight risk to quality the trade-off for much lower costs? And if lower costs affect increased profits, have businesspeople (in both the UK and the US) kept their focus on short-term profits over long-term gains? This is just what they themselves have criticized in the past!

Hackett sees this side of the picture clearly, as does the AFL-CIO, in its own way. The ability of workers to contribute to the economy is severely compromised by high unemployment and the creation of lower-skill/lower-paying jobs. Obviously, when workers do not contribute to the economy as consumers, products do not get made and job creation stagnates. Unemployed workers purchase fewer products. Houses lie empty when buyers have no money. This, you see, is a portrait of a deflated consumer-driven economy. When consumers feel insecure about buying, or cannot buy, the economy languishes.

Its opposite, the vibrant economy, relies on employers taking full advantage of potential workers. But the un- or under-employed can hardly do that, and again the economy takes a blow.

While disheartening, these facts are reality and to be expected. Think of all the "Kevins" out there in foreign call centers and other modes of industry that used to call the United States home. Businesspeople, expectedly, act in their own interests and those of their companies. Should we sic the government on outsourcing? As well being politically unviable, it's unlikely to work. Why? Well, if outsourcing were banned, more companies would move offshore completely, and again, out goes the baby with the bathwater. And due to treaty obligations, we would find it difficult (if not impossible) to ban imports of that now-completely-offshore company's products. So, the process of outsourcing is going to continue.

In my opinion, the answer to this dilemma is a combination of three factors: 1) There must be an awakening of corporate consciousness. In other words, we must rely on corporations to take responsibility for their actions within the communities in which they serve. So the idea of terminating jobs in local communities to then create jobs in foreign countries could be considered irresponsible. 2) Governmental intervention is required to encourage the reverse process. Providing incentives to keep jobs here or at least stagnate the exit of potential jobs will help promote corporate responsibility. 3) Consumers must support companies that promote jobs retained and goods made in the US.

Only by dealing with reality head on will we find solutions to the above-named dilemmas. There are ways for the government to offer meaningful help and create positive reasons for jobs and production to remain stateside. Even more significantly, go straight to the source and look to small business and *their* strategies for keeping jobs at home.

There is one exception to the consideration of offshore outsourcing: our immediate neighbor to the south, Mexico. Our northern neighbor, Canada, had similarly high production costs to ours and they are perhaps our largest trading partner. And while a strong Canadian economy is in our national interest, Canadians do not need American jobs.

Mexico, on the other hand, is a very different story. Our southern border is a leaky sieve where estimates of illegal entry approach 13 million, nearly equal to the populations of New York and Los Angeles combined. Our open border has become a national-security and political issue. Many illegal immigrants come in search of a better life, others to cause harm or just live off the fat of the land. Either way our public services are stretched to the breaking point, while life in Mexico improves not at all. Is it utopian to imagine a Mexico where undocumented immigrants are able to stay home and work for a decent life in their own country? A mild amount of Mexican outsourcing can be seen as relevant to this point, but so could thriving small businesses south of the border.

For good or for ill, outsourcing is a reality. And that is what economic policy makers must confront.

RECENT OUTSOURCING TREND

Outsourcing is often perceived as jobs and industries being exported to other countries, reducing the volume of available jobs here in the US. While this remains true, what I have observed in recent years is a relocation of workflow from one region within the U.S. to another, where the business climate is less prohibitive and more business-friendly, i.e., offering lower taxes, business incentives, and fewer regulations.

I have witnessed this happening all too often in New York State. Although we're considered to be the financial capital of the world, and most businesses enjoy the prestige of having a New York flagship store or office, this comes at an extremely high price to their bottom line. So what do they do? Move the portion of their non-key talent to other states where the business climate is more sustainable. Is New York losing its brand?

The answer is yes and no. Yes, because we need to attract retail business and industry to our state by lowering taxes, reducing undue burdensome regulations, and providing incentives for small businesses. No, because we will always be a beacon of hope and a lighthouse for the world to admire and visit. But we must strengthen our economic infrastructure in order to maintain our brand as a thriving economic capital. We have to become competitive with other business-friendly states like Texas, where taxes are lower and the business climate is more pliable.

TECHNOLOGY VS. MANPOWER

A final issue in the current economy is the fact that technology is rapidly replacing manpower, as many longstanding industries and jobs are becoming obsolete. Think of factories that once employed hundreds of employees, now operating with a fraction of their former staff while robots replace scores of workers.

Technological growth abounds, particularly in the realm of communications. Indeed, H.G. Wells, the author of the 1895 science-fiction classic, *The Time Machine*, would not recognize the slowness of today's physical travel, as opposed to what he so fantastically predicted for the twenty-first century. One outstanding example that comes to mind is the huge success of the lumbering, reliable Boeing 747 (in service since 1970, the civilian outgrowth of the 1946 B-52 Bomber) over the glamorous, supersonic Concorde passenger plane. While the SST has gone the way of the Model T, the far slower 747 keeps on flying.

However, physical travel isn't as necessary when communication is instant and easy. Should my firm want to open a

London office, I can handle most of the discussions via telephone, conference calls, webcams, texts, and email. I can even read my emails on my smartphone, and communicate with potential partners en route to lunch. While an in-person meeting may occur with British partners at the end of the process, it will be more ceremonial than anything else. I may even exchange signed original documents instantly, as they are scanned and sent as PDF files beforehand. Were the celebrity-laden Concorde still running, it would be infinitely worth the enormous savings of a longer trip on a 747 for that in-person meeting, all paperwork having been handily accomplished electronically.

Communications alone do not account for the only way technology has changed our work processes. Perhaps you are reading a hard copy of this book, or perhaps you're reading it on a Kindle or Nook, electronically scrolling through the pages while hoping not to miss your bus or train. I edited this manuscript on my iPad. So what has become of the vast operational workforce once hired to publish, assemble, package, deliver, and sell millions of copies of books and magazines each day? What about the small businesses that supported these products—the store clerks, managers, buyers, and sales teams who make up bookstores and major publishing houses? I'm afraid many have been displaced. Hence, we are witnessing entire industries becoming obsolete or rapidly evolving as manpower loses ground to technology.

There are good arguments to sway writers in favor of this new media. For one thing, it has increased the demand for good copy; for another, what writer of your acquaintance demands cash money for royalties? Payment by electronic deposit is another convenience no one would forfeit. Paper is saved with e-readers, and the computers used by writers today do not compare to the Royals of yesteryear, with their endless mess of typewriter ribbons and lack of portability. So clunky messes have been replaced by efficiency, again eliminating jobs that were once vibrant and secure with more reliable tools to aid the writer. A good thing for our society? Absolutely; but invention of new sustainable industries must come into play in order to support the workforce that has been made redundant.

Technology improves productivity, and is likely to continue. So isn't it better to adjust to the inevitable rather than fight it? Particularly when it has made our lives so much easier.

Unfortunately, it costs us, too, in terms of jobs. Take a look at manufacturing. From the beginnings of the Industrial Age through the mid-twentieth century, large industrial companies and manufacturers hired thousands of workers to assemble the pieces of products as well as the products themselves. Many people spent their working lives on the assembly line, retiring comfortably when the time arrived. Then came the onslaught of automation, and people were replaced faster than you could press a button. The savings in money and manpower were inarguable. And while people were still needed to operate the machines, soon computers came along with the same capacity, at enormous savings. Computers don't need health benefits or retirement funds, either. They don't call in sick or take vacations. So a lot of people were thrown out of work…especially people who were under-educated and untrained for anything else.

So bring on the training programs, right? They are certainly a sound method of fighting unemployment brought on by increased mechanization and productivity. But at the end of 2010 it became harder for government to afford these programs. And no wonder; raising taxes to pay for them is not only politically anathema, but also questionable from a purely economic perspective. And as laid-off workers from 2008 and 2009 paid fewer taxes in 2010, tax income itself decreased. State and local governments were facing major problems of their own in 2011, from the same problem of decreased tax income.

Throughout history, taxation has never been popular. It has even rung the death knell for many a leader who hoped otherwise. According to the historian Laurence Bergreen, in ancient times Kublai Khan won support from the Chinese by promising lower taxes.[23] Was he a member of the Tea Party Mongol Express?

Decades ago I thought that published books would exude a romantic appeal, especially those that are dog-eared and full of personal annotations. Bibliophiles would ensure their survival. However, though books are often the best agency in conveying in-depth information, they are not the best way to convey immediate information. The Internet has taken over in that area. If bad weather or any other factors confine you to one place, the Internet fills in, instantly providing all necessary information, be it weather, news, history, statistics, and databases of every kind. No trip to the library or newsstand is necessary; no need to get up out of your chair.

With libraries themselves devoting more and more space to electronic media and less to periodicals and similar publications, is it any wonder that these institutions are seen as less useful and viable, and therefore heading the list for budget cuts, if not obsolescence?

We've all carried magazines and books around, especially those of us who are regular commuters. We've gone from hard copies to laptops in a short period of time, sometimes chafing at the weight and innate fragility of that expensive little computer. Now the aforementioned Kindle and Nook have arrived to accommodate daily reading, and for more you have only to turn to the iPad, upon which you can not only store reading materials of every kind, but also access the Internet to check the stock market or catch up with old school friends on your email, engage in social media, or have a pleasant game of solitaire. And you can do it all in privacy.

So while we readers are now accommodated handsomely, newspaper and magazine publishers are hemorrhaging red ink. Publishers have responded by offering electronic versions of their publications, but this comes at a price. They have downsized the numbers of hard-copy staff. Writers and editors, photographers and art directors in media have a good chance of making the change to electronic media. But what about the others? What about typesetters? Newspaper delivery people? They've seen their jobs become nearly obsolete. This scenario is stretched across many industries, from manufacturing to financial trading, and many others.

Recently I was returning from a trip to Syracuse late on a Tuesday night. As our car approached the tollbooths, I noticed there were eight of them, completely void of personnel. In fact there was an electronic sign flashing that read, "Please slow down to allow cameras to take photos of your license. You will be billed for this toll." Immediately I thought these were the jobs of eight people working second shift at one time. How unfortunate that this is not the case any longer. But on the other hand you rationalize this change by saying, well, it means streamlining the cost of running government, thereby saving taxpayers a few dollars. So what about the people who were displaced? Do they collect unemployment, go back to school, and develop new skills, or do they become part of the underemployed?

Some highly visible companies may make a show of continuing to employ people whose jobs are on the way out; decreasing staff by attrition is always better PR and easier on current employees who live in fear of the dredded pink slip. But look to the future and ask yourself, who will be taking those jobs? No one. And no one can expect a company to hire future workers for non-existent jobs. While technology has saved businesses money in a variety of ways and have provided efficiency to our lives, the cost of an eliminated, untrained workforce will only continue to make itself felt, and felt painfully.

THE MODERNIZATION OF THE U.S. GOVERNMENT

While major corporations are not the same as a governmental body, there are lessons to be learned in the way corporations constantly evolve in order to remain competitive in a dynamic global economy. Their goal is to provide a unique product or service that will appeal to their target audience, at a cost not prohibitive to maximizing the total gains to its stakeholders. This means consistently finding new and improved ways to provide that maximum profit.

Of course the government's agenda is quite different, but reducing spending, creating a healthy business environment, and providing the relevant services needed to provide national security and other programs that support local communities are its chief priorities. However, in order to achieve them, certain benchmarks must be set, along with a full re-evaluation of the system. We talked about corporations reducing overhead in order to remain competitive—which comes at a price to our economy in terms of lost jobs and industries. And yet, these corporations thrive and succeed. What does this tell us?

Government needs to consolidate departments and eliminate redundancy, fraud and waste, while ensuring accountability for how resources are managed to its constituents. This means, after careful consideration, downsizing departments that overlap and eliminating altogether those departments that are ineffective. The modernization of government will come at a short-term cost with long-term dividends as a whole.

Most importantly, all of government—city, state and federal—must work cohesively to bring about the results, at a cheaper cost to taxpayers.

Interstate commerce must be a priority, by ensuring that a business in one state can do business in another with a one-stop shopping deal, to be explained later. After all, though one country, we're composed of fifty different states. We need to seriously create and provide a platform that allows small businesses ease in moving or expanding from state to state. This platform includes:

➤ Centralized computer application at a one-stop protocol.
➤ Elimination of redundant departments to streamline
   efficiency.

> ➤ Creation of team environments to accommodate group discussions for improved efficiency and lateral participation.
> ➤ Use of the computers and the Internet to provide truly efficient, consolidated data in one central location, e.g., businesses of the same type, geographical research data about products and trends.

Some departments (like the SBA) need to either evolve or be eliminated outright. Sound draconian? Not necessarily; there is a proficient way to save the SBA if done correctly. In order to be relevant in the new economy, the SBA must reinvent itself as an invaluable, relevant resource and advocate for small businesses across the board. Unfortunately, this is not currently the case most of the time.

I have had my share of frustration with the SBA; so have many of business owners with whom I've spoken. Several decades ago I was really excited about starting my business. I had carefully formulated a strategic business plan, but was lacking enough funds to pursue my endeavors. I learned about the SBA while earning my Bachelor of Science degree in Business at Brooklyn College. I was so excited, not only about presenting my plan, but about requesting assistance in securing a loan. Upon arrival I met with a counselor who after a series of questions and a brief glance at my plan told me that it wouldn't work and that my business would fail within the first two years. How discouraging and daunting that was, coming from a source that should have been encouraging and supportive! Well, that was twenty-one years ago. I started my business out of my home to reduce the overhead cost. For the first few months I worked as the salesperson, recruiter, bookkeeper, and receptionist. Eventually the business gained sufficient traction that I was able to hire my first staff member, and that process continued until the end of my first summer in business. I knew it was time to move into our first office space in Manhattan. By then I had a permanent staff of eight people and dozens of temporary workers onsite at client locations. Within the next few years, what was a home-based business started on a shoestring budget grew into a multimillion dollar corporation hiring thousands of people, with major Fortune 100 corporations as clients and governmental agencies in our portfolio. What if I had taken the advice of the SBA counselor? Fortunately, entrepreneurial spirit is stronger and deeper than the discouraging words of a few. That's what has made America a great country: the pioneering spirit of "can do" attitudes.

5

REGULATION AND BIG BUSINESSES VS. SMALL BUSINESS

Are Small Businesses an Afterthought?

Overregulated or underregulated? Without doubt the biggest argument of the past thirty years has the pendulum first swinging one way, then the other. For better clarity, a recent history of the economic crisis characterizes the debate as follows:

> *Arguments about economics seem arcane, but they never change much. They are usually between those who advocate government intervention, on one hand, and those who argue that free markets operate better on their own, without government. Boiled down even further, these arguments are largely those about the issue of human rationality versus irrationality. One side holds that markets are basically rational and efficient on their own—that they are an optimal way of societies to allocate resources—and governments only interfere. The other side holds that markets and the people who make them up often behave irrationally, inefficiently, and therefore the best course is to keep government involved at all times.*[24]

In effect, I have both arms raised because each argument has its strengths. Straddling the fence? Not a chance. The pro-regulatory position tends to believe that non-regulative markets exploit workers. To avoid such oppression, markets must be totally controlled, bringing us back around to Marxism, a philosophy unsuccessful when put into practice.

The problems inherent on the other side of the regulatory debate have been all too visible during the past two years, with massive numbers of layoffs and foreclosures. A giant like Enron did not fall due to being overregulated; quite the opposite. But too little in the way of guidance and control has its own dark scenario: anarchy.

Neither side of the arguments seems to bear in mind the reality that financial markets are unique in their behavior as compared to other markets, such as those in products and services. Markets, after all, are run by humans and thereby susceptible to the same human foibles. While some people's consciences are in fine working order, others leave much to be desired. And neither trait is connected to ability. The managers in the sub-prime mortgages demonstrated the case of ability in one area, deficit in the other, i.e., lacking moral judgment. This is not even considering criminal behavior in that market, seen in the forging of signatures on loan documents, something which came to light only after the bubble had burst and the foreclosure signs had gone up.

So what is the answer? There is a concept of enlightened self-interest, which is insufficiently understood. If people help others while helping themselves, their winning does not depend on another's loss. If taken further, the market will expand and allow both parties to gain. Had only Wall Street bankers and investment firms seen the limits to how much profit could be safely attained from one particular source, could not disaster have been avoided? But with growing deregulation, mortgage derivatives were less likely to provoke federal government intervention. Red flags were ignored. Investors were so pleased with their returns, they didn't look up to see the storm clouds gathering.

On the other hand, direct government interference is an emergency measure only. Most individuals are not out to rob banks or other people. Thankfully there are police for those who are. Regulations, therefore, need to act like police in a democracy, ignoring us when we behave, but intruding rapidly to enforce sensible laws (that serve a clear purpose) when we do not.

Both sides in the regulatory debate have gone astray and erred in the same area: their focus is on big business alone, and putting all of our eggs in that one basket works only as long as the basket doesn't get dropped.

SMALL BUSINESSES AS JOB CREATORS

The federal government defines a small business as one with under 500 employees. In 2006, according to the Bureau of Labor Statistics (BLS), the employment split was 60 million workers employed by companies of under 500 employees, with another 60 million employed by business of 500 and above. This division has been more or less stable for the past several decades.

The SBA took a sharp look, in March 2010, at the impact small businesses have on jobs.[25] This federal-government agency discovered a truth which should have been exposed much earlier.

The majority (95 percent) of all business start out with fewer than 20 employees. But even under a normal (i.e. pre-Recession) climate, new businesses have a more difficult time getting bank funding than more established firms. That means 90 percent of all businesses will continue with only 20 employees. The SBA weighs in accordingly:

> *The fact that most firms start small is not surprising, as the resources needed to launch larger corporations are tough to come by at the outset of a new venture. What does seem surprising, however, is that few startups grow by more than a few employees.... Most small firms start small, stay small, and close just a few years after opening.*[26]

The thing is, small businesses still tend to create the bulk of new jobs, with the subsequent job destruction upon closing. The following table shows clearly how, despite the high casualty rate in small businesses (with resultant job losses), small business still manages to add a net gain to job creation. Take a look.

JOB FLOWS IN ESTABLISHMENTS BY EMPLOYMENT SIZE OF FIRMS, 1993-2008 (millions of jobs)

SIZE OF FIRM	NET CHANGE	JOB GAINS FROM		JOB LOSSES FROM	
		Openings	Expansions	Closings	Contractions
Total	20.7	105.2	398.3	97.7	385.1
Less than 20 employees	4.6	54.8	104.5	51.5	102.9
20 – 499	8.7	11.5	150.6	12.6	140.8
500 +	7.5	1.0	93.9	1.3	86.0

The above table illustrates unequivocally the need for, and great value of, providing financial and technical assistance to small businesses not just before but *after* their operations have begun. This would have the obvious effect of expansion-driven job increase and a reduction in job loss from possible closings and market contractions. Imagine comparable figures ending in 2006, before the Great Recession threw a wrench in the works of job creation at all levels.

Here are some statistics to bring the point home. The Bureau of Labor Statistics shows that some 17.9 million net new jobs were created between 1993 and 2009; "net" indicating created jobs versus destroyed jobs.

➤ Firms with under 20 workers are credited with 22.4 percent of new job creation.
➤ Firms with 20-499 workers are credited with 42.8 percent of new job creation.

➤ Firms with 500-plus workers are credited with 34.8 percent of new job creation.

Interestingly, in one of those mysterious statistical anomalies, no less than the Census Bureau offers conflicting figures. It states that in the same period as referenced above (1993-2006), 25.1 million new jobs were created, with firms of under 20 employees being credited with 72.1 percent of new jobs, firms with 20 to 499 employees credited with 16 percent of new jobs created, and firms of 500 or more credited with 12 percent of new jobs created.

What are we to make of these numbers? What are we to make of the different numbers supplied by different bureaus, aside from different time periods and different methods of defining small business? One pattern emerges clearly:

➤ The BLS figures show 65.2 percent of net new jobs created by businesses of under 500 workers.
➤ The Census Bureau figures show 88.1 percent for the same group.
➤ The table shows 64 percent of net new job creation by small business.

Not to beat my point into the ground, but the bottom line is that the majority of the 100 pennies generated in our economy comes from the creation and growth of small businesses.

This is a major source of job creation. Also interesting to note is that the greater job "turbulence" comes with firms (making up only half of all employment) below 500 employees. It is worth repeating: this is a major source of job creation.

In the words of the SBA report:

While small and large firms provide roughly equivalent shares of jobs, the major part of job generation and destruction takes place in the small firm sector, and small firms provide the greater share of net new jobs. In some ways this role as a major creator and destroyer of jobs is a result of being the major creator and destroyer of business in general. The term for this in small business research circles which was popularized by Joseph Schumpeter...is "creative destruction."

David Birch...discovered that the end result of small businesses' creative destruction was a net increase in employment....[27]

In addition, small firms...tend to fill niches in the labor market that are underserved (often have high rates of unemployment, for example). Small firms employ higher shares of Minorities than large firms (65.9 percent of Minorities work for firms with fewer than 500 employees). And compared with large firms, small firms also employ higher shares of individuals with low educational attainment—a high school degree or less (63.2 percent); high school-aged workers (63.8 percent); individuals 65 or older (64.6 percent); disabled workers (59.4 percent); and rural workers (64.3 percent).

My more than two decades of working with large corporations, especially high-end investment type firms, further supports this point. Big businesses prefer to hire young, fresh Ivy League graduates to join their workforce and deliberately seek out such people, especially for product-related management positions—in other words, high-profile jobs that deal with detailed analysis, client interaction, market exposure, etc., which eventually lead to promotions into managerial positions, repeating the cycle all over again. Most candidates for employment who fit these criteria are non-minority, of more affluent backgrounds. With the change in government regulations most companies are forced to comply with EEOC policies ensuring that inclusion and diversity is a part of their corporate culture. But to what extent is this effective, and is it just a public-relations ploy to satisfy the Jesse Jacksons of the world?

There is a clear conviction here, regarding small business as the major job-creation arena. It is summed up: "With the labor market struggling in recent years, small businesses are a logical group to look to for job recovery, as they have such a large role in job creation."[28] High-impact small businesses, such as Dell and HP, are most likely to grow and create jobs. As noted in a previous chapter, in professional business vernacular they are called "gazelles."

When you think about it, it's hard to think of any behemoth that did not start out as a small business and eventually become a gazelle; Ford, General Motors et al., had to start somewhere and were not born the fully developed enormous corporations they are today. That is not to say that the goal of every small business is to become a giant. Other gazelles that come to mind, at least in their initial conception, are Starbucks, Blockbuster Video, and of course Apple. A new way of operating computers was Microsoft's specialty, one that revolutionized the world. With Apple, we saw the popularization of personal computers. When surpassed by Dell and HP in the desktop computer realm, what did Apple do but strike out in a new direction and become the leader in hand-held devices such as the iPhone, iPod, and iPad, so that it seemed like their products were generations ahead of the competition. Their customer service centers are not called "Genius Bars" for nothing.

Starbucks took one of life's staples, coffee, and repackaged it, replacing plain old java with latte, and did it through thousands of smaller establishments worldwide, both franchised and directly owned. Sound familiar? You're probably thinking of the golden arches, and indeed McDonald's was probably the first such corporation to mass-distribute a common product, in their case hamburgers. Both hamburgers and coffee had been around for ages. And while you'll not find much variety at either Starbucks or McDonald's, you will find a brand built on a convenient, reliable, consistent product sold at a reasonable price.

Remember the excitement of the original VCRs? The novelty of watching the film of your choice in the comfort of home was seized upon by Blockbuster Video, which organized mass rentals of movies. Much of their market, in the wake of improved DVD technology, has been lost to Netflix, who found a better way to mass-distribute DVDs, first by mail, and now by video-streaming for an instant entertainment experience.

What do Starbucks, McDonald's, Blockbuster Video, and Netflix have in common? They all started out as small businesses that grew into high-impact companies—gazelles. Unlike the majority of small businesses, they had their fingers on the public pulse from the outset and foresaw the way things were going. Even Blockbuster had the rug pulled out from under it by Netflix. Home delivery trumps a trip to the store every time, as does a new way of marketing a traditional product. The constant evolution of technology, and our need to create new sustainable industries, is rapidly becoming the number-one solution of this book.

It is worth tax dollars to assist the net addition of jobs from the minority of small businesses that survive (even if they don't grow big) by providing viable support and funding for such firms. This is investment that makes sense in the truest form of the word. Government spending, after all, will yield more return in total tax dollars than the amount spent. While the SBA was designed to offer such programs, they are sadly lacking in efficiency and effectiveness. One area that illustrates this is the all-important loans. As the agency itself expresses it on their website, "the SBA doesn't directly offer loans to small businesses, (but) they do provide...a number of different resources and opportunities for finding small business funding." That last part translates into a complex boondoggle of differing information that rivals the worst excesses of the IRS. Again, a *centralized* (and publicized) information source for small businesses is desperately needed.

Small businesses' greatest strength, as seen by the above-mentioned corporations who started out small and became gazelles, is found in innovation. It is essential to assist small businesses with this component—and not just developing new ideas, but putting them into action. Innovation is our country's greatest asset, product, and export, starting from small companies growing to become giants and everything in between. Therefore we must acknowledge small businesses with concrete assistance.

SMALL BUSINESS AND INNOVATION

Back in 1985, the legendary management expert Peter Drucker spoke eloquently on this subject. He wrote that:

> *Innovation is the specific tool of entrepreneurs, the means by which they exploit change as an opportunity for a different business or different opportunity. It is capable of being presented as a discipline, capable of being learned, capable of being practiced. Entrepreneurs need to search purposefully for the sources of innovation, the changes and their symptoms that indicate opportunities for successful innovation. And they need to know and to apply the principles of successful innovation.*

A recent report on small business and innovation expressed forcefully and in further depth the interdependence of both when it concluded that:

In the next decade, small businesses will embrace innovation even more broadly than they do today. Passionate owners with deep market knowledge and an entrepreneurial spirit will adopt new methods and business processes to increase productivity, grow their business and save time. They will take advantage of a wide range of new technologies to improve their products and services. And their agility will let them create new business models to seize new opportunities, improve their competitive position and provide more value to their customers.

In the shorter term, innovation will help small businesses and the U.S. economy through the current recession. Small businesses react quickly to changing economic conditions and their owners have a can-do attitude, enduring and even creating opportunity out of adversity. Despite the tough times, the vast majority of small business owners remain upbeat about their long-term business prospects....

Innovation will be mandatory for small businesses over the next decade as they survive and thrive by seizing new opportunities, improving their competitive position, and providing more value to their customers.

Small businesses are up to the challenge. They are natural and continuous innovators. Small business innovation takes the form of smaller incremental or market-sustaining changes as well as business model shifts and even market-changing innovation. These innovations result in improved products and services, better business processes, increased customer value and stronger financial results.

Most small business innovation focuses on the commercialization of new ideas, methods and processes and not patentable, scientific research. Because of this, the impact of small business innovation is often overlooked. But despite being silent innovators, small business success hinges on innovation and is an important driver of economic growth.[29]

INNOVATION DESPERATELY NEEDED

How many areas can you think of as practical fields for small-business innovation? How about energy? Take a look at the following illustration of our current energy sources in the United States.

CURRENT ENERGY SOURCES IN THE UNITED STATES

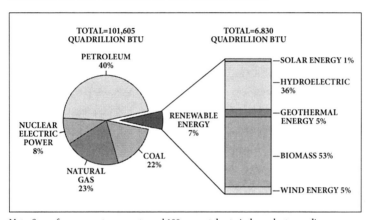

Note: Sum of components may not equal 100 percent due to independent rounding.
Source: EIA, *Renewable Energy Consumption and Electricity Preliminary 2007 Statistics.*
Table 1: U.S. Energy Consumption by Energy Source, 2003–2007 (May 2008).

As you can see, 85 percent of our energy (much of it imported) comes from hydrocarbons. Although the issue of global warming remains controversial, it is widely understood that hydrocarbons are injurious to the environment. Fossil fuels are finite, though when they are actually going to run out is debatable.

Other countries, notably Denmark, have been in the forefront of the development of alternative energy sources. As far back as 1981, the Danes were a leader in waste-to-energy solutions,[30] and remain so today. We need not only to emulate their example, but to take the lead in marketable, small-scale energy technology and an increased use of garbage burning to produce energy. How about something like a hydrogen fuel cell without the

hydrocarbon fuel source? At the end of the day, energy development is an international issue and its solutions will have to
reflect that scope.

The United States, no longer a leader in inventing energy
technology, has been taking the back seat not only to Denmark
but to Japan. The Japanese have developed a home device for
recycling waste material. (Small business alert: a product that
would produce fuel usable in the home would surely turn a nice
profit. It could be something as simple as a device to crush paper products and render them safe to use in connection with
a hot water boiler. Tax credits would encourage the inventor.)
Laws could possibly be enacted requiring power companies to
purchase any excess power that homeowners feed back into the
power grid. Owners of solar panels are already enjoying such
benefits. Why not spread the wealth?

What about the larger small businesses? They too can be inspired to find new ways of producing their own power, with
economies of scale unavailable to homeowners. Without doubt,
given their broader scope of resources, they could invent ways
to reduce economies of scale to a smaller level.

According to *Alternative Energy News* (www.alternative-
energy-news.info/technology/garbage-energy/) a number of
companies are already using waste to produce energy, including BMW (by recycling methane gas), TransPacific Energy,
and others. They do this both directly and indirectly—through
co-generation, i.e., using otherwise wasted energy, such as the
production of electricity using steam from an industrial process,
or the use of steam from electric power generation as a source of
heat. This is not only good public relations, it is good sense, and
most of all good business. For example, take a look at Cox Interi-
ors, a producer of wood for interior decoration in Campbellsville,
Kentucky. After 25 years in business, Cox is graduating out of
small-business staffing levels. Part of its manufacturing process
produces some 100 tons per day of waste wood.

When local jurisdictions began to regulate and limit land-fills, Cox sought ways to develop waste-disposal alternatives. These included mulch (for agriculture) and several methods of burning. Co-generation, the most appealing, would also produce heat and cooling for Cox. Since operations for the Cox waste-to-energy plant began in 1994, the firm has been amply able to meet its own energy needs and even enjoy a bit of profit by selling off excess to the local utility company. Cox not only saves several million dollars a year, but ecologically disposes of wood waste.

Would such a scheme benefit a really small business? No. This is where regional innovation centers come in. Think of Silicon Valley in California. Such centers can also be found in Boston and Northern Virginia. In Part Two, I will discuss how such centers provide an attractive advantage for foreign companies looking to relocate to the US. A small-business production park would be an ideal solution for several small businesses to resolve their collective waste-disposal problems. Most office waste will likely be burnable for co-generation and there you have significant savings on waste disposal costs.

Areas other than energy can be examined through small-business innovators. Combining agribusiness and energy, they can develop or invent other ways to produce ethanol than with corn. Sugarcane bagasse is used extensively in Brazil and could be tried here. In addition, it is certain that other bio-mass alternatives are just waiting to be discovered and put to use. Small-business innovators can also develop new methods of food production in tougher, and increasingly warmer, climates.

While 70 percent of our planet is covered by water, one of the most obvious needs is cheaper ways to perform the desalination of ocean water, rendering it fit to drink. It could go a long way in reducing the amount of plastic-bottle waste, too. Alternatives to hydrocarbon exist, and safe drinking water will offer a far more valuable commodity.

NASA technology has transformed so many aspects of our lives, from solar panels to medical advancements, especially in burn treatment and anti-aging skin products. Companies working to develop private-sector space travel are growing closer to making it commercially viable, if only to the few very wealthy prospective space travelers. These companies are either small businesses, or just on the cusp of big business.

Whoever succeeds in inventing an inexpensive method of scrubbing the smoke from burning hydrocarbons (in factories and motor vehicles) will be the next Bill Gates, in terms of personal fortune. While it is still necessary to locate substitutes for these substances, the United States has an estimated several hundred years' worth of coal beneath its soil. Liquefy it, and we could phase out deep-sea petroleum and dispense with Arctic drilling. Sound utopian? So did space travel once upon a time. And we could make a huge dent in global warming—both as scientific threat and political issue.

The United States can be restored to its dominant place in the world economy by a greater support for inventors and small businesses. At the same time, major political and social problems would be effectively addressed, while those inventors and businesses could achieve great wealth.

If the phrase "venture capitalist" is entering your mind right now, we are on the same page. The above criteria define the vantage ground for such individuals who understand the risks involved in "nothing ventured, nothing gained," and are prepared to investigate and follow through on new innovations. "Venture" can also be seen as a place for governments in search of ways to expend tax dollars to best advantage in terms of job creation, improved economy, and increased tax dollars in return. But consider this: before government can become a true friend to business, it must relinquish its role as facilitator of, cavalier corporate recklessness.

SMALLER AND LARGER BUSINESSES: HOW DO THEY RELATE TO EACH OTHER?

Large businesses are often dependent on smaller ones to supply products or services and smaller businesses rely on that client/vendor relationship to sustain their existence. Thus, they form a symbiotic relationship. A perfect example of such a service is the one I provide as a workforce capital management company, which incorporates staffing services within our basic offering, a business I created in 1992.

Staffing services are an evolution of employment services. The idea of an employment agency, charging a fee to people to find them jobs, dates back to the 1890s, a decade which suffered a severe economic depression as a result of the panic of 1893, due to railroad overbuilding and subsequent bank failures.[31] Unemployment ran over 10 percent for five years, reaching close to 20 percent in 1894, far surpassing the Great Recession of 2008-2010. The 1890s were distinguished by increasing industrialization in the U.S. and a negative balance of trade. Immigration brought on an early form of globalization, as the period from 1890 through 1910 saw the largest migration to the US, relative to the American population. It is easy to see how the employment agency added flexibility to the labor and employment landscape, by having professionals handle the job search for workers, and also facilitated employers by presenting the best possible candidates for positions.

The staffing service as we know it today was born at the end of World War II, during the industrial wind-down and demobilization as troops returned home. William Russell Kelly founded the oldest staffing agency in the country, now known as Kelly Services. The difference between the staffing service and the employment agency is that the former charges the employer for supplying workers, while the latter charges the employee, generally upon being hired. Also, the employment agency seeks to place permanent hires, while the staffing agency concentrates on both temporary as well as permanent placements. Temp-to-perm is more popular in today's tough economy, giving the employer and worker a chance to try each other out without making a full commitment. The advantage to the employer is in an immediately filled position along with the convenience to wait and see about full-time hiring. The employee of course gets immediate employment and increased economic power, instead of enduring a period of idleness while job-hunting for a full-time position.

The majority of staffing and employment agencies are likely to be small businesses. But from whom do they get their business? The answer is, a variety of companies; however, large firms are more likely to need huge volumes of workers than a smaller company. And the larger firm will likely have more repeat business, not to mention longer-term projects. Also, the larger firms usually have offices in other states outside of its main headquarters, with desks waiting to be occupied by temporary workers as the need arises. Understandably, relationships between staffing agencies and large corporations develop, and the staffing agency will be in the position to expand its own base by opening more offices, or forming partnerships with other such agencies. The staffing trend in the new economy is for large, global corporations to employ full-time temporary employees indefinitely in non-key positions, because it's a cheaper overhead cost, and a temporary workforce supports a quick downsizing of staff without affecting the public relations of the company or shaking shareholders' trust. This trend has proven to be cost-effective and allows large corporations to save millions of dollars on full-time labor, diverting the employment liability and payroll costs to their suppliers.

6

GOVERNMENT
VERSUS BUSINESS

Having examined the need for a level playing field for business and government, I cannot overstate that government needs to function as an ally to business, not an obstacle. Indeed, it is one of several recurring (and interrelated) themes of this book. Just look at all the businesses fleeing (to name one example) New York State for greener tax pastures elsewhere, and it is easy to see government as an obstacle to overcome.

Business, however, has to play fair, too, and government must function as an ally to ensure that it does. Too frequently, government alternates between negligence and heavy-handedness. Neither is working.

Examples abound worldwide of governments seeking the proper balance. Adam Segal, the Ira A. Lipman Senior Fellow for Counterterrorism and National Security Studies at the Council on Foreign Relations, has explored this in his book, *Advantage: How American Innovation Can Overcome the Asian Challenge* (W.W. Norton 2011). Using the analogy of the "smart grid" for the type of economy and climate for innovation the government needs to establish, he contrasts it with the "dumb grid," a term for normal electric distribution. Electricity, in the dumb grid, has no way of storing its unused portions. (Some adjustment is possible in states where solar-power users can sell power back to the grid.) The system can also be partially cut off in the event of an emergency, to prevent systemic collapse. Power can additionally be purchased from a neighboring system. However, if anyone recalls, as I do, climbing down nineteen flights of stairs in the summer of 2003 when such a collapse occurred, the nomenclature "dumb grid" really comes into its own. A sizable portion of the northeast U.S. and southern Ontario, Canada, was blacked out. And it hasn't only happened here—a few months later, all of Italy (save the island of Sardinia) suffered the same situation.

By contrast, a "smart grid" permits more vigilant monitoring and control of the distribution of electricity, as dictated by need and/or circumstance. Segal calls for the same method in encouraging innovation, adjusting our policies to adapt to and meet changing needs and circumstances. A smart grid in a world of globalized innovation monitors what is going out—specifically, what technology is flowing from the United States to Asia and how it is being utilized—and what (and who) flows in, i.e. what is coming from Beijing and Bangalore into the United States. Rather than alienating friends, it means developing the infrastructure and the incentives for innovators anywhere in the world to plug into our grid…and not only that, but inserting people into place to take advantage of the new world of decentralized innovation (distributed generation).[32]

The smart grid of innovation and invention also means facilitating other people to join and contribute to the grid.

There is one vast country currently exemplifying the advantages of reform. And it is considered one of the world's rising powers. The country? India.

India presents a good example of succeeding in overcoming problems and in seeking investment.[33] It did not happen overnight. Just a few years ago it ranked poorly on the "ease of doing business" scale created by the World Bank and the International Finance Corporation (IFC). Starting a business in India:

- ➤ Requires 11 procedures.
- ➤ Takes 71 days on average.
- ➤ Costs 62 percent of one year's income.

Equivalent figures for China are:
- ➤ 11 procedures.
- ➤ Takes 48 days on average.
- ➤ Costs 13.6 percent of one year's income.

Indian business organizations have emphatically stated that excess regulation of entry and exit into a business is a major problem in attracting both outside and internal private investments. They have watched the U.S. economy carefully, learning from our successes and profiting from our failures.

But India has always shown consistency in its treatment of foreign investors and domestic businesses. "One of the paradoxes of India's policy regime is that few restrictions apply to foreign-owned enterprises and not to Indian-owned entities, yet the perception remains that business activity is over-regulated and foreign investors are viewed with some suspicion."[34] A second study reports that:

> *Although foreign investors frequently complain that their business activities are over-regulated in India, the fact is that very few restrictions and regulations apply to foreign investments that do not also apply to domestic investments...India still generally extends national treatment to foreign investors...though national treatment hardly provides for a painless and straightforward process for foreign investors unfamiliar with the complex permitting requirements and government approvals required to develop a power plant in India.*[35]

In 1991, responding partly to a major economic crisis and partly to World Bank and IMF pressure,[36] the Indian government undertook extensive efforts at economic reform. "The Indian economy underwent a basic transformation starting in 1991, when the government of the day decided to make major structural changes in response to an acute foreign exchange crisis and other difficulties in economic development. Sporadic attempts in the 1980s had produced unimpressive results. The country's rulers embarked on a course of dismantling the "license raj" (rigid government control over production and distribution of manufactured products) and greater integration of the Indian economy with the global trading and investment system."[37]

India does not yet rival China as a major "Asian tiger." The Indian economic advance has followed a bumpy road, encountering such shocks as the Asian currency crisis of the late 1990s and the disastrous relationship with the notorious Enron. However, India does have a substantially improved economy which continues to strengthen.

Unfortunately, we sometimes show our own "license raj" in this country, particularly on the state or local level, something I learned while seeking to open branches of my office in states other than New York. The experience is best described as counter-logical.

SMALL BUSINESS AND LOCAL BUREAUCRACY

The difficulties inherent in establishing a small business in several cities across the nation can be mind-boggling. Going into business is hard enough in itself, and the odds are always stacked against the brave souls who try. They want to accomplish each step legally, remain in compliance with various legal regulations, and they want to get it right. Registering for and learning about the various state and local compliance issues can be daunting. Such matters as workers' compensation, unemployment, and any particular licensing or filing necessities for that state, county, or city are anything but straightforward. Depending on the industry, every state has different laws and requirements, with a hodgepodge of disjointed information that is nigh on impossible to uncover. If you are a small-business owner with limited resources and manpower, this can serve as quite a deterrent to expansion or growth. Larger companies with a full legal department are more equipped to handle these irregularities as they vary from state to state. Attorneys are on hand to research and complete the various legal compliance issues necessary.

I have my own experience in dealing with the cumbersome bureaucracy of local and regional governments, along with the disconnect that exists among them. Several years ago, someone from the Department of Consumer Affairs entered our office and requested to see our license. Fortunately I knew that she was mistaken, since staffing agencies do not require a license, but employment agencies do. The key difference is that:

➤ A staffing agency is paid by the client company who hired the employee.
➤ An employment agency is paid by the placed employee.

Wrong business! How many small-business owners with staffing agencies or other types of businesses may have gotten similar visits or citations and simply paid the fine, or unnecessarily applied for a license without proper counsel or access to accurate information? The expert from the state did not know this fundamental specification, but I did my research before starting the company and was conversant with the requirements. I offer the story as a perfect example of how confusing it can be for small-business owners to navigate the compliance issues within a state if resources are limited. The key is to have a centralized system of application and access to resources, where a business owner can safely fulfill all the necessary requirements for city, state, county, and local governments without missing key components, or being non-compliant.

I don't mean to condemn the Empire State, either. My company has been doing business just across the river in New Jersey for twelve years. About eight years after opening our office, lo and behold a missive came from the state attorney general of New Jersey, informing us that we had failed to fill out an application with his office and were therefore not in compliance with New Jersey business regulations. This came as news to us, since it isn't done in most states, and was never mentioned to us when we applied to the various state and local governmental agencies in New Jersey. Was it unreasonable to think we should have been told during our research and inquiry process? Apparently so.

But guess what? Had all the application documents been centralized, this could have been avoided, making it easier for a small-business owner to follow an online process covering all the necessary requirements by the state's law.

If that's not painful enough to consider, many counties within the same state require a separate registration in order to conduct business within that county, as I've experienced in my journey across the country. Fortunately, New York City, comprising of five counties, does not require that.

These are all robust arguments in favor of letting prospective businesses know exactly what is required, in detail, from the very beginning. Each state can have different requirements for doing business within that state, as in the previous examples. This means business owners must conduct a ton of research and get all the facts before proceeding, or hire legal counsel to assist with the process, which can be costly, especially for those with limited resources on hand. Government is big and obsolete, which makes it inefficient for the end user trying to access valuable information. Massive reforms must be made in order to update systems, centralize information, and create a more efficient and modern system of government. After all, corporations constantly revamp and readapt in order to remain competitive. So should our government.

TAXES AND OTHER DETERRENTS

Nothing is certain in life but death and taxes, and taxes will always be a factor in attracting business, with no taxes being the ideal situation. At the very least, taxes should be kept as low as possible when encouraging new businesses. Logical, isn't it? Unfortunately government, like the people who comprise it, do not always behave logically.

Specific taxes (when their necessity is validated) should be cut when possible. In addition, procedures and regulations must also be closely examined to prove *their* necessity. State officials have got to be cognizant that, in today's electronic economy, if a business owner finds raised taxes unjustified by lowered taxes elsewhere, she will vote with her feet on where to locate all or a portion of her business.

Such government actions go on the "con" list against opening a business in that state. Taxes, after all, are a cost—a negative for both government and taxpayers. Raising taxes has political consequences and economic repercussions as businesses seek a more tax-friendly, pro-business environment. Therefore any tax-raise needs to be balanced by offering positives in exchange. Ask any small-business owner considering which state to open (or expand) their enterprises.

In 2010, downstate New York introduced an MTA payroll tax to help with public transit. With its rate of .34 percent, small businesses pay $3.40 for every $1,000 of payroll. If an annual payroll is $100,000, that means only an extra $340 worth of tax per year (plus the burden of an additional filing). An employer's tax that directly benefits public transportation (and indirectly the environment) is hard to find fault with. But the question lingers: was this tax fully thought out? A lot of people outside of Manhattan—on Long Island and up along the Hudson Valley, where MTA service is minimal or nonexistent—emphatically say no. Again, new taxes are not always the way to go.

Attracting business to a state automatically brings in new jobs. The state then gains tax income from the hires (many of whom may have relocated). More houses will be built, bought, and sold, and more apartments rented. More money will be spent as consumers go shopping for goods and services, in general, all of which enriches the state's coffers.

Thinking outside the box, in the same manner that companies have a sale drive to attract customers and move merchandise, a city or state can have a small business drive to attract new companies. Let's think for a moment about Nevada. Suppose the Silver State were to promote this idea for six months and in so doing attracts 10,000 new businesses from neighboring California, or that these businesses have simply started fresh. And suppose Nevada does not levy an income tax on these businesses for the first two years. Now suppose instead that state imposes a minimal annual fee of $200 per year—unlikely to provoke resistance. Bingo, the state has just added two million dollars in additional yearly income. It may not seem so much, especially when compared with yearly budget in Washington. Even so, at a rough estimate of $2,000,000 per year for 10,000 newly attracted businesses, the state could allocate resources to developing its infrastructure, improving public services, and even providing incentives to attract more new business.

Don't most states have personal income or sales taxes from the money the new employees spend? So, by investing money in foregoing some business taxes, Nevada (or another state) will be repaid handsomely.

While in some ways this may seem an ideal scenario, the actual numbers would not be too difficult to achieve. A careful examination of regulations and taxes by governments might just yield surprises. While they're at it, it wouldn't hurt to have a close look at the full implications of the "full faith and credit" clause of the United States Constitution, Article IV, Section I: "Full faith and credit shall be given in each state to the public acts, records and judicial proceedings of every other state."

Looking at New Jersey again, this state should accept a New York business license as evidence that the firm meets certain requirements to get such a license in New York. Should New Jersey have additional requirements, what could be easier than asking for additional evidence of compliance with the unique New Jersey requirements?

For another example, Washington, D.C. makes it more difficult to open a business than does Arlington, Virginia, just across the Potomac River. Downtown Washington is accessible by foot from parts of Arlington. Check out a map and you'll see that much of Arlington is closer to downtown Washington than other parts of the nation's capital. There is also an excellent regional subway system, which, unlike New York's, connects to the suburbs. With a slightly different fare system in place, you can still walk to the subway from many parts of Arlington, take a fifteen-minute ride downtown, and walk to government offices. All this is to illustrate that states should apply logic to their business requirements, warranting (to the degree possible) that they are not more stringent than nearby accessible jurisdictions.

Another example can be called upon here in Arlington's favor. Washington D.C. law requires that the agency will have to pay for a temporary employee's sick day. However compassionate this may seem on the surface, it is not sufficiently thought out, is it? While paid sick days augur well for an agency's reputation and good-standing in general, they also add a new burden in terms of requirement. And an additional requirement hurts the agency, hurts the customer, and adds another reason to walk (this time literally!) over one of the bridges to Arlington or Alexandria, Virginia. You say Washington is a more liberal jurisdiction? Well, guess again. Arlington and Alexandria are as blue as they come, and Fairfax County (easily accessible by the Metro) comes close. I tell you all this to emphasize that it is not political. Virginia (like nearby Maryland) simply shows a better conception of how to attract business.

How well government is actually doing its job has to take precedence over the need for logic in business requirements. To continue with the above example, Arlington is convenient to downtown Washington, but downtown Washington is even more convenient to itself. Most everything is within walking distance, with no Metro necessary. Yet the issues of public safety must also be examined carefully, and if the business area is not sufficiently protected from crime, fire, or natural disaster, business requirements do not figure prominently. Washington, D.C. is now considered not just the hardest jurisdiction in which to do business, but the most dangerous, and can hardly compete with Virginia and Maryland.

Topping the list of worst states for small businesses is Washington, D.C. Our nation's capital has the second-highest corporate tax rate income, behind Pennsylvania, as well as high personal-income tax, individual capital-gains rates, and corporate-gains taxes. The Washington, DC area also has high property taxes added tax for S Corporations, high electric utility costs, an imposed estate tax, and a higher crime rate than the fifty states, according to the SBE Council.[38]

REGULATIONS AND PROCEDURES: DOING THE RESEARCH

Even more fundamental than complying with procedures is finding out that they exist in the first place. No amount of cursing or complaining can take the place of actually knowing what you're up against. And finding out can be a problem, particularly in a city or jurisdiction whose region crosses state lines. Again, I wave the banner for a central clearinghouse of small-business information, examined in more detail in Part Two of this book. As we have seen, Washington welcomes daily commuters from Virginia and Maryland, New York from Connecticut and New Jersey. Any business in these areas has its work cut out for it in multiple, particularly in the areas of state regulations for employment and unemployment insurance from other areas.

Any new businessperson has to find what the costs and regulations actually are, before deciding the good or ill of doing business in a particular area. Would you buy a shirt before knowing what it costs? Or a car, or a house? Neither would I. And if the very act of finding out proves too time-consuming and costly, you not only won't find out, you'll *get* out, and find a place more business-friendly. Also, if the prospective businessperson finds it too difficult to uncover simple requirements for opening a business, or strikes an avalanche of complicated requirements, he or she will be far less inclined later to give government the benefit of the doubt should some policy disagreement arise.

Prior to the Great Recession, no one ever consciously wanted to waste money, but it was a lot easier to sail close to the edge of carelessness. One lasting effect of the Great Recession is surely a deeply increased concern with the value of each nickel, dime and penny. And if the government finds it so hard to tell you—the prospective businessperson—what you have to do, how good are they going to be at doing what *they* must do? This can be a terrifying proposition, given what's at stake in committing to your business. Larger companies hire attorneys to help navigate the legal channels but most small-business owners, especially startups, do not have the budget to allocate such a cost. The additional expense of legal counsel would not be necessary if the mere act of finding information for a business to be compliant within each state was easily accessible or centralized.

As you know, I've opened branches of my agency in Florida and New Jersey, and expanded our service to several other states across the nation. The first step in most areas was the local Chamber of Commerce, a private-sector organization representing the interests of local businesses and the community as a whole. They are, as you would assume, meant to be promoting business development in their area, as it is in their best interest to do so. Indeed, their goal should be to promote their city and attract new businesses, residents, and investors. Therefore, the key function is to provide statistics, logistics, demographics, etc.

Chambers of Commerce also serve a quasi-governmental function as coordinators of information. In the case of my proposed expansion, I should have, in the best of all worlds, been able to count on the Chamber of Commerce for:

- ➤ Local and state requirements.
- ➤ Confirmation of government-supplied information.
- ➤ The inside story on opening a business in their jurisdiction.

But most could supply none of the above, nor provide a portion along with generic information obtainable online. Most of the representatives simply did not have sufficient information on what was required by the local jurisdiction as well as by the state.

Another important component of the collective information pool is Workers' Compensation. Most insurance carriers require a minimum payroll of at least $50,000 a month to supply coverage—far above the means of many a small business. I'd add to my information-clearinghouse wish-list easy procedures to obtain such insurance from a pool, in addition to general liability insurance and health-care coverage. This not only provides relevant information but a reduced cost for those expense items.

In the long run, gathering needed information in each city and state was unnecessarily daunting, far more than it needed to be. There was no one-stop clearinghouse where one could identify, and arrange to meet, all the necessary requirements for setting up a business. Neither city nor state seemed to know what the other was doing. Unfortunately, from a "cost to government" perspective there is no way of measuring these negatives in terms of discouraging new-business owners; no way of measuring the cost of that loss to the economy as a whole.

Part Two

SOLUTIONS

7

REVIEW OF THE ECONOMIC REALITIES
OF THE 20TH CENTURY

Ironically, the gain from the current recession, for all the troubles it has created, will leave us open to new growth to a degree unprecedented in any of the recessions we have endured since the Great Depression of the 1930s. Sometimes a new broom sweeps clean, and the potential for our economy to bounce back better and stronger depends on the lessons learned during the Great Recession of our time, along with the strategies we have implemented to steer the course toward economic prosperity.

If we look at the Great Depression of the 1930s, defense spending led the way out of that calamity, increasing when Britain (along with France, Canada, Australia and New Zealand) declared war on Germany in September 1939. President Franklin D. Roosevelt anticipated America's eventual involvement in World War II and understood the need for preparedness. Public opinion, primarily isolationist until Pearl Harbor, made it necessary for FDR to move slowly. While in some ways we were unprepared for the December 7, 1942 attack, in terms of the materials produced we were far more prepared than we might have been.

World War II is often credited as ending the Depression. FDR's economic measures are credited, rightly I think, with saving the free-enterprise system in this country, and perhaps even democracy itself, given the concurrent rise of Communism. The economic improvement was, in a sense, subdued. "In 1941, still officially in a peacetime economy, America produced more steel, aluminum, oil and motor vehicles than all other major countries together. The problem was how to turn this abundance from the purposes of peace to those of war."[39] The United States was not politically ready to switch to a wartime economy, let alone enter the war. As late as 1937, neutrality legislation made it difficult to prepare for war. It was not until 1942 that, aside from naval expenditures, war production was truly under way.

A similar situation occurred in the late 1940s. Remember the Cold War? A recession had occurred in 1946, at least partly due to reduced defense production and the massive numbers of men leaving the military to re-enter (or enter for the first time) the job market. Then defense production had to step up quickly in response to the Cold War, and remained a highly significant economic factor until the 1990s.

While our current challenges may, in some ways, resemble those of the Great Depression, we are unlikely to see expansive federal rescue legislation in the foreseeable future. The current federal deficit will not permit it. And as perilous as the threat of terrorism may be, it does not endanger our very existence in the same way that World War II or the Cold War did. Nevertheless, we do face major challenges, particularly a change in the essential nature of our economy.

WELCOME TO THE NEW ECONOMY

We're living in an age in which technology is rapidly replacing manpower as the economy swiftly changes. The world economy is truly becoming a global village, as countries like China and India gain a strong economic foothold to compete with and challenge the United States' economic power. Many fields—such as telecommunications, media, government, manufacturing of big-ticket items, and pharmaceuticals—are seeing particular changes, as increased individual productivity leads to vanishing jobs.

The recent closure of Borders Bookstores is another example. Consumers are relying on easy and increasingly efficient ways of living their lives as emerging technology stimulates the desire for change. So what are we going to do about this?

Small businesses have been hit the hardest as globalization of products and services are forcing a higher level of competitiveness than before. Businesses are working twice as hard to achieve half the profits, compared with the pre-recession period. The cost of running a business has increased, with taxes, regulations and healthcare reform. This is going to take a toll on the hiring decisions made by companies in future. Healthcare reform, although necessary, will come at an expensive cost to the economy, and especially hard hit will be small businesses.

While traveling around New York State recently, I met with a small-business owner in Plattsburgh. At the time he had fifty-eight employees working full time at his car dealership. His long-term goal was to expand his business to other locations and hire an additional seventeen employees in an area of the country that desperately need jobs. Unfortunately, in light of new regulations springing from healthcare reform, he is reconsidering pursuing his expansion goals in favor of downsizing his operations, so that he can maintain a staff of fewer than fifty workers. Think about how this reverberates throughout the nation as business owners are hit with additional overhead costs that ultimately reduce their bottom line. Who suffers? Hard-working Americans.

As small businesses struggle to regroup and survive, they are now given the undue cost of doing business imposed by new laws. Outsourcing, downsizing, automation, streamlining and terminations are all going to be a part of future business models if we do not pay attention. Forcing a leaner workforce means fewer jobs available as free enterprise is stifled with prohibitive costs.

We will see more independent contractors surfacing who cannot find work on account of shrinking jobs. These contractors will be educated workers unable to gain desired employment, working solo or in clusters, trying to make a substantial living.

A large portion of the downsized workforce will be undertrained and unable to gain employment. The responsibility will lay on the shoulders of these workers to further their education and training, or rely on government to provide solutions to this dilemma.

The awareness that our economy is rapidly evolving is crucial for us as Americans to recognize. It's not going to be like the last recession, because we're literally going to have to reinvent ourselves. This is completely unfamiliar territory and we must be prepared to proactively engage in this emerging economy.

8

AN ACTION PLAN

In this section, we will examine ways around the problems of attracting new business, whether from out of state or from budding local entrepreneurs. The plan, as you'll see, calls for several steps to be undertaken by state and local governments, as well including a role for big businesses to play in social responsibility. We also look at the necessary solutions for small-business success in the US.

A CANCELLED INVITATION BECOMES A PLAN

The train of thought that began with my White House invitation, continued after that invitation was rescinded—and, with a lot of free-associating along the way, eventually became a plan. My ideas, which had taken hold too deeply to dismiss, became razor-sharp, fully fleshed out, and integrated. By focusing on the areas of slowest growth and snowballing up from there, the plan will get things rolling in a big way toward long-term growth and stability in the small-business sector; a sector which is, after all, the very backbone of our economy.

My thoughts had evolved into a clearly defined business model (that could also work as a political strategy) which would:

- ➤ Create a National Centralized Business Resource Center that would support businesses and modernize government.
- ➤ Create sustainable jobs and industries.
- ➤ Get smaller businesses moving.
- ➤ Streamline and restructure an obsolete government to save taxpayers money.
- ➤ Encourage and support invention on a grassroots level.
- ➤ Buy government more benefit of the doubt.

TAKE THIS JOB AND MAKE IT

As discussed earlier, industries that were once thought to be invincible are rapidly becoming obsolete as technology replaces manpower. So what do we do—pretend this isn't happening and wait for a revelation? No, we need to proactively address these issues and provide viable solutions that would deliberately move our country forward.

Our mission must be to create sustainable new industries that will take us into the new economy and beyond. In so doing we must encourage and support invention, especially at the grassroots level. There are brilliant minds waiting to be nurtured and discovered. Our future depends on creating enough private-sector jobs so that everyone who wants one will have one, improving their own lives and society in general. Training programs for the unemployed and underemployed will yield tremendous profit as these people meet the new job requirements of an increasingly technical society. Expensive? Maybe. But compare it to the costs of the unemployment roll and the lack of income generated from tax revenue to the government. Hence, we will be repaid abundantly in:

➤ Savings on entitlement programs.
➤ Reduction in the unemployment rate.
➤ More foreign businesses attracted to our economy on account of skilled labor.
➤ A more vibrant economy as consumer spending increases in all sectors.

NATIONAL CENTRALIZED BUSINESS RESOURCE CENTER— THE TOOL

My goal in writing this book is not only to outline the problems as I've seen them in my twenty-five-plus years of business experience, but also to provide viable solutions that can create a discussion to help move our stagnant economy forward. The focus of this book has been on small businesses, but in reality my solutions will benefit business in general. At the end of the day we're all Americans, and no one profits by anyone's losses.

It might seem safe to assume that a state or city would make it as simple as possible for a new business to set up shop, whether it's a completely new enterprise or a branch of an already-existing business from out of state, but this isn't the case. Government regulations, due to their nature and the ground they must cover, will always be formidable. But what a difference in the business landscape, were government to make it easy for all business owners to find out what exactly the regulations are, through a centralized, easily accessible online reference interconnecting not only federal, city, county and state, but all fifty states (and the District of Columbia) as well. I call this a National Centralized Business Resource Center (NCBRC), where information and requirements pertaining to doing business in each locale are readily available in one place, simplified and easily accessible. This would help improve interstate commerce by providing a more effective vehicle for small businesses to navigate the complexities of doing business nationwide, making it easier to start or expand a business while being compliant with federal, state, county and city regulations.

For this to work successfully all the states would need to work cohesively to formulate a national database specifically designed to provide information regarding doing business in each particular state, as well as all needed applications to ensure business's compliance with the diverse rules and regulations within that geographical region. The federal government should take the lead in this project, assimilating its information and applications into the program. I call it one-stop shopping because it saves a businessperson time and money by being able to find everything in one location, including information on that particular state's business-compliance issues. You might say, why not just link all the states' websites to this one database? Well, the trouble is that some states are ahead of the game in providing easily accessible information, but most are not. Information is confusing, inconsistent, fragmented, or on multiple sites within one state. For example some states require that a new business file with its attorney general's office, the city government, and the state, and secure a license, all from different sources, whether it's online or via a request through email. It's time-consuming and discombobulating for someone who just wants to bring his/her idea to the market, and in so doing stimulate the economy.

Centralizing information will save businesses and government money. It will save potential businesspeople enormous amounts of valuable time setting up or expanding their operations. Taxpayer dollars will be saved as government manpower can be focused elsewhere. In addition, compliance issues will be more effectively tracked and managed with fewer errors. Remember, if I want to open a business, the time I spend on the phone, emailing or visiting different government offices all adds up to taxable income. By the same token, the government official I am speaking or meeting with or the person answering my email is also getting paid. It is costing the government for me to expend the effort to piece together each bit of information

The centralized information system would have a multifaceted purpose. In addition to providing an all-inclusive application and resources for businesses, augmented portals would provide a national database of job titles and average regional wages based on categories, skill sets, experience and geographic location. This would provide consistent information across the board that would set a benchmark to guide employers based on regional standard wages, and employees would know what is reasonably acceptable.

With teachers, police and firefighters being laid off left and right, could not government money be better spent elsewhere? Think of it: all needed information, including the proper definition of job titles, business forms and other requirements, can (and should) be easily available in one place.

Among other advantages, the creating of such a National Centralized Business Resource Center would constitute superb pubic relations for the government, something it desperately needs, especially from the small business community.

This function will fall under the jurisdiction of the Department of Consumer and Business Services. By revamping and improving the SBA to provide a more streamlined access to resources and information, this department can now have a more efficient role in providing beneficial services to the business community across the board. The cost to taxpayers? Nothing. And the savings to the government will show in the millions of dollars freed annually by eliminating inefficiency, time, and money spent on countless hours of customer service by both government employees and research by business owners.

This idea also improves interstate commerce and encourages a small-business owner located in one region of the country to pursue business opportunities in a different region that may never have crossed his/her mind if this centralized resource center was not available. The end result is that thousands of mini-gazelles will be formed all across the country. How awesome is that? This will facilitate true interstate commerce efficiently, as foreseen by the Founding Fathers when they were writing the Constitution.

NCBRC—MANAGED SERVICE PROVIDER

We've talked about the National Centralized Business Resource Center as a tool to assist entrepreneurs in facilitating their legal business requirements and accessing pertinent information online; but what about taking it one step further and becoming a conduit for information flowing to businesses? For example, governments could provide information networks linking new ideas in need of funding with venture capitalists seeking ideas to fund, and promote this information via the NCBRC. Yes, venture comes from the same root as *adventure*, but let's reduce the risk—make it less a matter of luck than of design—that ideas and money join together. This online information center will also assist potential entrepreneurs in finding the venture capitalists they need for mutually beneficial (and lucrative) partnerships, making the NCBRC one of the largest networking resources for businesses worldwide.

As a Managed Service Provider the NCBRC could also:

> ➤ Help the private sector build a technical network of "best practices," demonstrating how to do things. Especially important will be advice and assistance in developing and marketing ideas. Look again to the Founding Fathers and see that the Constitution itself was a product. *The Federalist Papers* (a collection of essays authored mainly by Alexander Hamilton) were marketing the product to win state, government and popular approval.

➤ Promote and encourage the creation of small-business
   cluster networks operating cohesively across the country,
   allowing each cluster to complement the product/service
   provided, thereby increasing their market share and
   growing the businesses exponentially. For example, an
   accounting firm in New York connects with a business
   consulting firm in Chicago and a computer software-
   production firm in Los Angeles to form a mini-cluster
   of three businesses, basically selling services to similar
   markets/clients. The benefit for the three businesses
   is expansion of their services to two additional states,
   targeting clients that are already in place—an amazing
   opportunity that would be quite difficult to accomplish
   if one firm were to pursue all three markets alone. Think
   of this cluster multiplied many times over, combining
   complementary products and services…how amazing
   would that be as a new way of expanding your business
   across state lines into an unfamiliar territory, with the
   resources and backup of a cluster partner with brand
   recognition already established in that particular state?

➤ Increase knowledge of assistance programs by public
   outreach efforts, not by just letting people know what is
   available, but helping them find out what they specifically
   need. One idea? Have SBA representatives hold town-
   hall-style meetings in different neighborhoods. In a
   city like New York, cast wide your net to include all five
   boroughs and the vast variety of neighborhoods therein.
   This gives small-business owners a forum to be heard
   regarding specific issues micro-targeted to their regions
   and industries, and achieves two things: first, bringing
   the federal government into our communities, thereby
   improving public relations, and second, helping solidify

and strengthen business communities by allowing access to informational and financial resources.

➤ Encourage government at all levels to target job development and training efforts to where they are needed. Why do a few communities sustain significant unemployment rates while there's a one-to-one ratio between total job applicants and total job openings? The most likely explanation is lack of qualified people for particular jobs. Solution? Promote and sponsor job-training programs and get businesses involved by giving tax credits to companies that hire and retrain employees who have been terminated as a result of obsolete or outsourced jobs.

Bear in mind that most outsourced jobs are not returning; neither are industries that once were vibrant. In all of the above suggestions, it is imperative to develop more sustainable jobs domestically, and to support the growth of current small businesses to make up for jobs lost to outsourcing and obsolete industries.

MILITARY SKILLS BENEFIT THE PRIVATE SECTOR

According to the *Washington Post*, the unemployment rate for returning Iraq and Afghanistan war veterans is slightly higher than for the country at large. While military skills do not always translate to the civilian sector, employers worth their salt should recognize that good work ethics such as reliability, loyalty and self-discipline, plus the ability to learn and adapt along with strong leadership skills, are highly prized assets in employees, and not easy to find these days. Many military personnel have served our country by helping to ensure the safety of our nation abroad, yet return home to find that the corporate and other sectors are less than willing to provide employment opportunities. Why are the unique skills of these returning veterans not more highly valued? Here's another opportunity for government intervention: providing tax credits to businesses with a veteran-inclusion policy that provides training and development for returning vets with a stellar record and a proven track record of personal growth.

TAX BENEFITS

It is advantageous for state and local governments, such as the state of New York, to consider decreasing corporation taxes to a reasonable level. This will attract businesses back to the state and encourage the formation of new businesses. This may seem counterproductive but it will more than pay for itself in terms of increased revenue, both from the high volume of new business and from taxes paid by a new and vibrant workforce.

In recent years there has been a migratory trend of businesses moving areas of operation from states with higher corporation taxes and greater regulations, to more business-friendly environments with lower taxes and fewer regulations. I've experienced this with my own company as major clients downsize hundreds of jobs within the city and then open the same jobs in other states that offer better business leverage.

How can government effectively reduce taxes and provide greater social services to its community? By first reducing its size, eliminating redundancy and waste while providing transparency to its constituents. And while a small business may not find it worth the move to another state to save on taxes, someone seeking to open a business from scratch may well indeed seek out the best tax breaks from other states. Without such an option, the new business may never become a reality, a situation that, when multiplied, reverberates nationally.

Thanks to the ability to do business online, a physical presence (in terms of an office) is not the necessity it once was. Companies can operate in various states without being physically present, provided they're in legal compliance with the various governmental requirements. This is an actuality governments may have yet to take into account when proposing tax and regulatory policies for business.

In addition, state and local governments should provide tax breaks to encourage inventors of new products and services, provided that they are viable solutions that create sustainable jobs with a proven track record. Invention has always been America's particular genius, and in today's economy we need to provide support for the next super idea. The Founding Fathers, when writing the Constitution back in 1787, even invented a country. Simply stated: give people a good understanding of exactly what they need to develop and market their ideas. As John Hancock himself said, "The greatest ability in business is to get along with others and influence their actions."

PRIVATE-PUBLIC PARTNERSHIPS

With more flexibility and less ideology, government will create more effective policies. For example, a stronger focus on small business by the government will neatly merge with a particular trend, glimpsed on and off for the past few decades. What I'm getting at now is the concept of private-public partnership, or PPP. Bringing government and private industry together for specific purposes, PPP allows each party to bring its own strengths to the table, in keeping with the overall précis of this book, and as illustrated by the story in the Introduction.

Just who brings what to the table? Well, government (particularly the federal government) offers a direct concern regarding general national interest and a broader perspective, along with coordination skills. The private sector discerns the most efficient means of operation. Meritocracy, wherein the selection/promotion of staff on the basis of achievement (rather than job tenure), is a private-sector specialty in complete opposition to the government model. With seniority rendered obsolete, one large obstacle to success is removed.

And—another exciting bonus—small businesses can *combine* to work in PPP together. After all, coordinating a project is not dependent on whether one large company or several small ones are involved. Is it substantially harder? No. Government can either do this directly or appoint one company to serve as coordinator for the smaller members. In this way, PPP actively promotes the spirit of innovation. While a larger company is carrying out a specific project, smaller firms can be developing new methods of task accomplishment.

Clearly, rather than an anything-goes-hope-for-the-best approach, PPP gives organization and shape to business modality, representing the safely monitored flexibility necessary to the restoration of an effective U.S. economy. Rather than the methods of getting jobs done, its emphasis is on getting the job done. The result? The bottom line—rather than endless debates over the role of government—will predominate.

9

CREATING NEW SUSTAINABLE INDUSTRIES

Creating new industries is priority number one for improving the economy and strengthening its infrastructure for the future. It makes it easier when a community has natural resources, which can be harvested and sold for a profit. However, when that is not the case, invention and creative solutions become the core elements of economic sustainability.

Currently, information technology (IT) is the fastest growing field of invention, as smart hand-held devices, smart televisions, and other electronics are constantly being upgraded, taking the technology to the next level of sophistication. Yet we're still using fossil fuel to power our vehicles, thousands of people die annually from starvation, and acres of rainforest are being destroyed each year to accommodate human consumption without regard to long-term consequences.

We are living in a world not of science fiction, but of scientific fact. More funds have to be invested in the research and development of the sciences. There are areas of physics and chemistry that are being explored, but the possibilities awaiting discovery are endless. There are areas that can revolutionize our lives, like nanotechnology, biotechnology, green and agro-technology, yet we have only scratched the surface of their potential. And very few people comprehend how much of this works, as it is accessible to a select few. Increased visibility in local community colleges through courses, lectures, workshops, and even inter-college competitions (similar to a spelling bee) would broaden the reach of these revolutionary technologies and allow creative minds from all backgrounds the opportunity to learn and to challenge themselves, and step up to the plate with the next new discovery.

ENCOURAGING NEW TECHNOLOGY

The risk with new technology is that if someone does not see the value of or need for it, chances are the idea will not move forward. Furthermore, if finding ways to service and maintain that product is challenging, the need for it further diminishes.

For example, the invention of electric cars—a wonderful idea, but we do not have an infrastructure in place to support it. For now, the driving range of these cars is limited to the capacity of a fully charged battery, and heaven help the driver whose battery runs out on the interstate. So what is the solution? There have to be "plug-ins" available at the local gas stations, street meters, along the highways, and at home to recharge the car while not in use. Or perhaps an inventor can develop a solar-powered rechargeable battery that's less reliant on manmade infrastructure and is thus truly independent, making the car far more attractive to a broader consumer base. Unfortunately, until these ideas are in place to support this technology on a mass scale, the appeal for such a product is very limited.

This would be an excellent project for small-business clusters, as previously mentioned, coming together and working toward solving this problem. With the support of government, and with a large electrical company partnering with small-business clusters, the potential for successfully developing this product further is enormous.

This is but one idea whose time has come—one example of a long-term, sustainable industry waiting to be further explored, realized, and capitalized.

THE MARCELLUS SHALE IN NEW YORK

The Marcellus Shale is an untapped source of natural gas that could sustain the upstate New York economy for years, and at the same time produce huge volumes of natural gas, reducing our dependency on foreign imports for decades.

A controversial element of this idea is that hydrofracking may pollute our water table and our environment in general, as has been the case in the past. However, with modern technology (and careful research and implementation) I believe that hydrofracking can be accomplished safely, effectively, and without major risks. It's impossible to characterize any process as completely risk-free, but mustn't we take chances in order to move our country forward? Look at the oil spill in the Gulf of Mexico that BP has been working to remedy. Think of miners trapped underground in Chile for months. The list goes on. While not advocating recklessness, I am saying that we have to take measurable risks to move forward economically.

I recently traveled to upstate New York and was stunned at the number of once-vibrant cities that are now ghost towns. Industries have moved out without being replaced by new ones. Some towns rely on the government for jobs—such as schools, prisons and military installations—but as I've mentioned time and again, the government does not create jobs, the private sector does. For each person hired by the government, we the taxpayers are left with the bill.

So what are we going to do with the Marcellus Shale? Fortunately, lawmakers in Albany are beginning to see the light as the options for viable sustainable industries are becoming limited and budget gaps are tightening. I say we think like entrepreneurs and capitalize on an opportunity by finding creative solutions to the problems. Here are some of the benefits to the Empire State and to the nation in general:

- ➤ Thousands of jobs created.
- ➤ Decrease in our dependency on foreign energy.
- ➤ Improvement in the U.S. economy, especially in New York.
- ➤ Lower taxes, restoring New York's traditional status as a business-friendly state.
- ➤ Revitalization of "ghost towns" into thriving communities.

REFORMING ENTITLEMENT PROGRAMS

Perhaps there was once, and still is to a degree, that emblematic slacker known as the "welfare queen." Aside from being a blatantly sexist designation, the breed (comprising both men and women) has largely reduced in number due to increased workfare programs and more stringent requirements for the collection of welfare. However, the problem at the heart of programs like welfare, and even unemployment, is their ability to accommodate a lack of motivation on the part of the recipients. Why look for a job when there's already a reliable check in the mail?

The unemployed who are capable of working fall into the main category, subdivided by the underemployed; those who have been unemployed within the past six months and are currently collecting unemployment, the unemployed who have been collecting unemployment checks beyond one year, and capable workers collecting entitlements indefinitely.

A focus on the basics of human nature will render it far easier to address the general unemployment problem. There is an alarming number of people, according to recent statistics, who, having "timed out" on their unemployment, have simply given up trying to find work. Either way, whether welfare lifers or timed-out unemployed, the best method for getting people to seek work earnestly is to increase the number of jobs, encourage training programs, and further education. That's obvious, right? As for welfare, work incentives have already proven successful and need to be proactively cultivated. And employers should be given tax incentives for hiring those currently on entitlement programs; likewise, government needs to reinvent and promote welfare-to-work programs, thus relieving the cost of the entitlement programs, an enormous burden to taxpayers.

Remember too that while unemployment payments are taxed, actual paychecks are taxed more. So what we are talking about now is government investment rather than payouts. Investment differs from entitlement or discretionary spending in that every dollar the government spends is returned several-fold in taxes or direct repayment of loans. That's a big difference.

Aside from political and human imperatives to assist the unemployed, this benefits the economy overall and revives business in particular. Our economy is a consumer-based one, and when people spend money, the economy grows. It is a fact that working people spend more money, and it's also a fact that the unemployed are becoming disenfranchised from the lack of economic growth while out of work, and therefore spend less.

For the unemployed and for able-bodied people receiving other entitlements, the government should create internships within federal, state and local departments that allow these individuals to keep their skills current, permitting them to remain marketable for future job opportunities. This in turn provides the government with manpower as these individuals collect entitlement checks, a better way of managing taxpayers' money. Let's face it: employers prefer talent with current work experience over someone who has not worked for the past year or more. This not only benefits the unemployed individual, but government provides the assistance necessary to help maintain the individual's skills *at no cost to taxpayers*. In fact, for each person hired, the tax burden on both businesses *and* individual taxpayers can be reduced. This gives new meaning to the expression win-win.

The longer a person is unemployed, the harder it will be for him or her to get hired; unfair, but true. Résumé gaps blind employers to what they're losing: experienced, mature, and talented workers. Unfortunately, with a high employment rate we have seen little in the way of concentrated effort to directly address this problem.

Another solution for those recently unemployed (and collecting unemployment) are back-to-work incentives. These will encourage thousands of people to intensify their efforts, with renewed enthusiasm, slaying the dragon of discouragement and reviving the traditional can-do spirit. The incentives themselves will be in the form of a back-to-work bonus payments after four months of continuous employment, be it full-time or long-term temporary. And not just employees will see the benefit; the same bonus will be given to employers hiring these new workers, enabling them to take risks more confidently and overcome apprehensions of the long-term unemployed. Workers hired under this incentive are likely to be valuable indeed, bringing new enthusiasm, hope, and excitement to the table, along with their own proven skills.

Government and corporate-sponsored internships will also continue for workers seeking to keep skills current through tough economic times, or possibly to transition into new industries as many people look to reinvent themselves in the new economy, The four-month benefit incentive would move the unemployed to seek work again. The cost to the government will be a fraction of what would be paid in unemployed-worker benefits for the full term allotted. The same four-month bonus would be in place, with employers benefiting from freshly trained, highly motivated workers with recent experience at a fraction of the cost of hiring a full-time worker. In addition, this will tie into the corporation's social-responsibility program.

More and more businesses are providing telecommuting programs for workers, which benefit single parents hoping to raise a family while collecting a paycheck. All of this benefits the government as well, by increasing the tax base. And it represents a cost savings to businesses. Still skeptical? Increased productivity can be measured by fixed matrices.

Such measures will affect individuals as well as groups and companies. Think of it:

➤ Getting the unemployed to work again.
➤ Galvanizing hiring with carefully designed initiatives to provide liberation from unemployment.

This will give the United States a crop of fresh workers as opposed to faltering unemployed. For the unemployed who may refuse to participate in such programs (without good reason), benefits might be reduced. However, in the short term, without hiring incentives in place, a wholesale cutting of people off unemployment is both cruel and detrimental overall. Millions of dollars would be taken out of the economy in a time of crisis.

Look at it this way: in the long-range outlook, constant renewing of unemployment insurance benefits only leads to stagnant growth. On the other hand, offering these workers an alternative, one that benefits both them and the economy, makes far more sense than simply extending benefits.

10

REGIONAL CENTERS

Throughout this book, the need has been specified for local and state governments to establish a climate that is friendly to business. For one thing, "fair" taxes on business may not always work as well as they seem to for governments. Consider a theoretical example: a state has 10,000 businesses, and taxes them an average of $10,000 per year, yielding a yearly income of $100 million. But—imagine if by lowering taxes to an average of $2,000, the state can then grow the number of businesses (by enticing small businesses with the reduced tax rate), to 100,000. The total tax income then doubles. Taxes are created to raise *total income received by government so that the needs of its citizens are effectively served,* not maximize taxable income from each business or person. That is what governments need to remember, even though the logic may at first seem counter-intuitive. This is not to argue that taxes should not be fair.

Furthermore, this is not an argument about the government's duty to spend money well, although I'm a firm believer in being fiscally responsible and conservative. The people will always want their money's worth and are quick to see when they're not getting it. In a working world that is increasingly virtual, relocating from one place to another is accomplished handily. And as we've seen, that is just what happens when businesses are not satisfied by conditions in one particular jurisdiction.

However, there is an intriguing confutation to that notion of the virtual working world. The Internet permits the exchange of documents across the country and around the world in seconds. A contract can arrive via PDF, be printed out, signed, and scanned right back. It is usually unnecessary for people to meet face to face anymore. But this does not explain why businesses frequently tend to cluster together—even the communications and electronics fields, the exact ones in the vanguard of new technologies.

Back in the days when communications were not instant, mature industries such as advertising and publishing were heavily concentrated in Manhattan. Businesses also chose locations that were best suited physically for their needs. The movie business originated in New York but moved to California for the space and climate. Factories first arose in Massachusetts where rivers provided power. The area most famous for its concentration of high technology industries is Silicon Valley, California. Recently, a new "media" district in New York City has adopted the moniker "Silicon Alley."

To create other Silicon Valleys, the "recipe appears simple and easy to replicate: concentrate universities, research institutes, and factories in the same area; build good schools, parks, and nice housing: offer preferential tax rates and financing to attract smart people and new companies; and eventually, so the theory goes, new clusters of regional innovations will flourish."[40]

Silicon Valley developed for a multitude of reasons. Almost a hundred years ago, it was already a (pre-high-tech) electronics center. Stanford University was founded there in 1891, as an Ivy League-level school, to provide an institution of learning equal to those that dominated in the East, and thereby prevent eastern exploitation of the west. Electric and electronic technologies, such as electric lights, telephones and radio were "coming on line" (to borrow a modern phrase) and the area's growth fed on itself.

In the post-World War II era, Stanford became firmly established due to an onslaught of students benefiting from the GI Bill, which permitted government-financed education for veterans. In order to accommodate all these new students, and the attendant facilities required, the university's leadership established industrial parks in the area. The management of these parks realized the need for legal counsel to provide appropriate guidance for new companies, along with venture capitalists to finance the new firms, and thus the die was cast.

The name Silicon Valley became synonymous with the software industry. While California taxes are not famous for being reasonable, and other areas, such as Utah, acquired high-tech areas of their own, Silicon Valley offered something extra—something that's been mentioned in these pages more than once: one-stop shopping for high tech companies. The San Francisco Bay area overflowed with superbly trained graduates from Stanford, Berkeley, San Jose State, and other universities. These same universities provided labs and recruitment facilities for potential employees. Financing and legal assistance for startups abounded. Product manufacturing, being outsourced, would not be more difficult than elsewhere.

New companies were also welcomed with the informal networking, business, and social contacts invaluable to any new enterprise. In-person socializing trumps its electronic counterpart any day. And if privacy is a major concern, it's a lot harder to electronically eavesdrop in person than online.

CONNECTING RESEARCH AND ENTREPRENEURSHIP

The words "innovation" and "invention" can be seen as interchangeable, and in many ways they are. From the perspective of job creation and economic growth, one seems to suffice as well as the other. However, there are differences to consider. Innovation specifies *new ways of doing things* while invention means *creating new things*. Viewed through that lens, the use of new inventions can be seen as innovation. We are safe in assuming they are steps in a process—i.e., create something new, then discover new ways of using it.

By far the best way to get innovations into use, and the best ways to create new jobs, is through entrepreneurship, found mainly in newer and smaller businesses. But capable utilization does not automatically follow creation. One recent report compares the case in New York City to that of Boston:[41]

> *The extraordinary level of research conducted inside the halls of New York City's universities and medical centers has produced some of the world's most rewarding scientific breakthroughs and scores of patented technologies. It has led to the development of drugs and commercial products that have improved the lives of countless people and resulted in hundreds of millions of dollars in royalties that have enriched the institutions. What all of this remarkable scientific activity has done is park the creation of a meaningful technology sector in the five boroughs.*
>
> *Regions with large and self-sustaining technology clusters are not created by luring the best high-tech companies from elsewhere, but by generating a consistent pipeline of homegrown technology businesses. Academic research institutions are by no means the only source for these new ventures, but they can provide a critical foundation, as cutting edge scientific research leads to a steady number of tech startups, often including enterprises with the greatest potential for growth. Perhaps the best example is MIT in Boston: according to a 2009 study, an estimated 6,900 companies founded by MIT graduates are currently located in*

Massachusetts; those firms employ just under one million people worldwide and account for 26 percent of the sales of all companies in the state.

Unfortunately, in New York, too many of the city's leading academic research institutions have lagged behind their counterparts elsewhere in spawning startup technology ventures from scientific breakthroughs achieved in their facilities. At the same time, the city's institutions have done little to ensure that companies that do emerge from scientists' research form and grow within the five boroughs.

The report goes on to speculate and analyze the reasons for this situation, citing one college official in particular who noted that the lower number of New York City startup companies could be blamed on one major element: the lower amount spent on basic research—a curious thesis, in light of the need for invention as the seed for innovation. Less money available for basic research is certainly a factor, but this is likely to effect all institutions to some degree.

The difference is not accounted for by numbers alone. Columbia University spent about half of what MIT spent on research in 2007, and launched twelve startup companies that year. But even if Columbia doubled its spending on research to meet MIT's expenditure, it would still take Columbia University a long time to catch up with its Boston counterpart—*287 years!*

Given the one example of Columbia and MIT, it is easy to see that New York City is out of step when it comes to commercializing inventions and developments. Why are New York universities not producing enough graduates with entrepreneurial fire in their bellies? Possibly it is part of the focus of universities on research, at the expense even of teaching. But this fault can be found at any large university. Universities vary, but I see very little reason to assume MIT professors have a more business-oriented mindset than those at Columbia. Reaction to past business involvement, and government contract, is also every bit as likely to set in at MIT as at New York universities.

The definitive dilemma is this: companies that are conceived and created at New York academic and research institutions, are mostly established *outside* of New York State. The report states, "The shame of this is that New York City frequently misses out on the tremendous economic benefits of technology startups that were created here. One missed opportunity is the jobs…."[42] As the report emphasizes, the majority of startup companies fail. Yet some do succeed. And that select few, those which are very lucky and very skilled, which grow and prosper, creating hundreds of jobs, benefit the city with taxes and locally spent money. These companies also create an entrepreneurial culture, which can light a fire under others. Some CEOs even specialize in running startup companies, for the exhilarating challenge as much as anything else.

With a high cost of living, high real-estate prices, and a shortage of space that can be used for commercial labs, reasons for the city's record vary. There is precious little indication of prolonged efforts toward the development of locally created technology in local businesses. (Normal office space will be hard to use for labs, with their extra power and water needs, and possible hazardous-material protections.) New York City, as I learned from personal experience (and outlined in previous chapters), can be a challenging place in which to establish a small business. It does not have a land-grant college, one of the practicality-based institutions arising from legislation passed by Congress in 1862, wherein land grants of 30,000 acres were given to states for the purpose of founding schools specializing in agriculture or mechanical arts.

To these reasons, factor in the belief, rampant in local academic institutions, that economic development is not their responsibility.

Don't they do enough already by bringing in students and faculty to live and shop in the local neighborhoods? The report points out the obvious: that it is hard to fault schools that perform in original research and education, but pay less attention to local economies than some think they might. However, "Considering all the assistance universities and research institutions solicit from New York City—preferential tax and zoning treatment above all—it is not unreasonable for city officials to expect them to do more to support the economy."[43]

What, if anything, are we to do about this situation? Is there really a need to correct it at all? From a national viewpoint, does it matter whether a graduate student with a degree from Columbia opens a technology company in New York City or upstate New York—or in Kansas? In many ways it does not matter on a national level, and the federal government would have no clear interest in helping a particular urban area, because job creation helps the nation anyplace it occurs. New firms can locate anywhere. One argument for supporting local startups is to avoid uneven economic development, wherein some areas prosper while others lag behind.

However, New York academic institutions, credited with producing pure science and technology the equal of any other city, generate far fewer startup companies. A startup in New Jersey, which creates jobs in New Jersey, might not help the big city across the Hudson River, but it does help the national economy. A startup not created at all, benefits no one.

The academic field, by its tenure-driven nature, is unlikely to attract people with entrepreneurial inclinations. But there are exceptions to every rule. For one thing, I am not including adjunct instructors who teach business and related areas at a college, or even at an adult-education level—though many of these instructors are likely to be people in business themselves, or retired from business with a desire to help others.

Some schools are notable exceptions, with strong programs to encourage technology transfer, better described as making technology practical.

The primary method used by schools is technology-transfer offices, which handle licensing of technologies developed at the school. "The most successful of these institutions have created programs that facilitate routine exchanges between scientists, engineers, and seasoned entrepreneurs, as well as a support structure whereby a would-be entrepreneur easily can get advice on various aspects of starting and running a business."[44]

Sound familiar? It should. My proposed centers would provide virtually the same services. A few things would be added, including putting potential businesspeople in touch with both funding and technology. Many successful startups that grew into world-class corporations—such as Apple and HP—brilliantly matched technology geeks with business whizzes. By the same token, my centers are designed to match invention and marketing.

The advantage my centers would have over universities will be in making it much easier to promote technologies from any source. They would be able to match all kinds of qualified people from all over the country. A university can be expected to promote technology development within its facilities, from which it can gain licensing fees. My centers can work with universities in their areas, as well as elsewhere in the country. Universities can be encouraged to cooperate by tax incentives, perhaps just altering the incentives they have. And when it is made clear that using my centers to find people to commercialize their technology will not cost them any money, watch encouragement blossom into enthusiasm. Universities can repay the services by offering themselves as sources of advice to budding entrepreneurs. Never was bartering so lucrative.

11

EMPOWERING THE
ENTREPRENEURIAL SPIRIT

Shimon Peres, the president of Israel, has been engaged in national and global politics since before Israel became independent in 1948. He is quoted in a book on the recent Israeli economic miracle as saying that, "The most careful thing is to dare."[45] I came on this quote while researching examples I might cite to develop and support my ideas.

Peres is an 86-year-old man who still looks to the future. He helped conceptualize, and then create, the Israeli aircraft and nuclear industries. He still stands as an example of what is called *chutzpah,* a term that has gone from the ancient language of Hebrew into modern Yiddish, and from there to colloquial English. *Chutzpah* is best defined as audacity, the willingness to try new things. It has undertones of a concern more for substance than form, which can lead to abrasiveness. The practical application focuses not on whether something can be done, but *how* it can be done. And it also has the implication of pulling it off with skill, care, and—yes—a certain bravado.

The Israeli military, for example, with a well-earned reputation of being among the finest in the world, is especially adept at using improvisation to identify and solve problems. (Ever

gone through the interrogation process before boarding an El
Al plane?) This is an adaptation to the basic reality that wars always contain elements of surprise and that battle plans often fall
apart. Hence the extensive and rigorous training, supplying the
needed technical skills to reinforce courage and quick thinking.

Israel's economic development in the last decade is credited
to different factors. But the most arresting element was that virtually all of them, with one exception, have also been true of the
United States at one point in our history, or remain true today.
The exception is the World War II Holocaust out of which Israel
was born, when, in May 1948 the Jews of Palestine, led by their
new Prime Minister David Ben-Gurion, declared an independent state in their ancient homeland.

Elementary to the Israeli economic ethos is a view, evolved
from its history, that not only can you succeed but you *must*
eventually succeed. Survival depends upon it. Their business
culture, in many ways unlike that of the United States, allows
for failures before ultimate success. It is a cliché (and therefore
true) to say that failure is necessary for success. Failure is only
preliminary to success if you learn from the failure, and keep
trying. Success also requires the ability to learn from success,
because it can come by accident. But—and this is crucial— success starts with the *belief* in success.

Most small-business startups encounter setbacks that can be
a valuable learning experience if one has strong determination,
although it may not seem that way at the time. Twelve years
ago my friend Robert started a small advertising company in
Manhattan. Within six months he made a fantastic business
connection while networking at a Harvard Club function in
Manhattan. His contact was the Senior Vice President of one
of the biggest entertainment businesses. With high hopes and
great expectations he opened a second office in Los Angeles in
order to establish a presence closer to his client and show good
faith. He hired a staff of five people and secured a seven-year

lease on eighteen-hundred square feet of office space. His intention was to also pursue other clients in that industry but none would be as lucrative as this single client. Within the second month of operation, after days of calling his contact, he finally got hold of him and was informed that the entertainment company decided to go with a larger advertising firm, that had a recognizable brand name and had been around for over thirty-five years.

Robert was devastated. He had invested all of his money in this second location at the expense of the New York office, which was struggling to survive. What had he done, he thought? The potential of losing the business was quite real, but he vowed to stay put and make the situation work. He began pursuing other contacts in the entertainment business, even promised to work on a few projects free of charge so that he could build a brand and reputation in LA. After a few months, he secured a few smaller contracts and within a year his business began to flourish as the larger accounts followed. Today he specializes in entertainment advertising and the bulk of his business is in Los Angeles. In fact, he became so successful there that the decision to close the New York office was practical. Currently, he has over twenty-four staff members, with average annual revenue in excess of fifteen million dollars and moved into a seven-thousand-square-foot commercial loft two years ago.

This is what happens when you don't give up despite failure, but learn from your mistakes and create a vision beyond what you may have even imagined.

When dealing with people, there is no 100 percent rule of behavioral psychology that applies to everyone all the time. But it is always fair to assume that success in any field is unlikely to be realized without ability in that particular field. Luck (or timing, if you prefer) plays a major role. One can do everything right and still fail to achieve an objective. Think of Danielle's story at the beginning of this book: she was a proven success in her field of public relations, yet could not fight a radically changing econo-my. It can even work the other way, though far less likely. One can make major mistakes and still succeed. The invention of Post-It notes comes to mind—a mistake that yielded millions.

One of the books I read as part of my research is *Start-up Nation: The Story of Israel's Economic Miracle,* by Dan Senor and Saul Singer (Twelve, November 2009), a book I highly recom-mend. Early in the introduction, the authors state a fact that I not only accept, but offer as an underlying core of my own book.

> *The economic downturn has only sharpened the focus on innovation. The financial crisis, after all, was triggered by the collapse of real estate prices, which had been inflated by reckless bank lending and cheap credit. In other words, global prosperity had rested on a speculative bubble, not on the productivity increases that economists agree are the foundation of sustainable economic growth.*[46]

The Israeli record of economic success provides the evi-dence that profound economic change can be achieved. Among the factors responsible is immigration. Voluntary immigrants tend to be people with a lot of initiative, passion, and the will to improve themselves, as well as dedication to the state of Is-rael. Israel was built by immigration, in this case people seeking not just improvement but escape from anti-Semitism. Many of these immigrants brought particularly strong technical skills, such as the 500,000 or so Russian immigrants in the 1990s, equal to ten percent of the Israeli population at the time. The equivalent would be for 38,000,000 such technically skilled, driven immigrants to arrive in the United States in this decade.

The military is another factor. Israel has compulsory mili-tary service—the Israel Defense Forces (IDF)—for both men and women. The Israeli military is credited as a training school, so to speak, for technological innovators. The military also teaches self-reliance and flexibility, and provides ready-made networks. The reserve-based IDF means that most people do not take the military career path. Instead, they seek an outlet for their skills, and have created a remarkable number of innovations and inventions. Israelis played major roles in developing, if not inventing, such procedures and technologies as drip irrigation and a major element that enabled the creation of laptop computers. By contrast, exceptional people in the American military are encouraged to stay in the military. They can look forward to a twenty-to-thirty year career. We certainly need good generals and admirals, but their skills are then lost to the civilian world. It is worth considering that, "What has typified the Israeli army throughout its diverse history is its commitment to innovation and its continuous maximization of the resources at its disposal, both human and technological."[47]

The United States has always been a country of inventors. The laptop computer, which the Israelis did so much to expand, recharges from an electric transmission system we developed. The ancestor of today's jet liners was invented in the United States, by two bicycle-makers who were also inventors and entrepreneurs: the Wright Brothers. Automatic rifles and machines guns, so necessary for Israeli defense, are American inventions. And if Israel has atomic warheads, we invented them too. As was mentioned earlier, the democratic system, which enables Israeli innovation to flourish, if not actually invented here, was introduced into the modern world by the United States.

What we can learn most from Israel today transcends a comparison of similarities between Israel and the United States. We should look at attitudes as well as details. For various reasons, the Israeli business and economic culture encourages innovation and invention. It inspires startup businesses and is much more accepting of failure than our business culture. Potential Israeli businessmen and businesswomen (with the skill and confidence of an IDF background) are above all encouraged to try.

This is one thing to which we have to return in this country: the desire for adventure. The first Jewish settlers in Israel in the 1880s had the pioneering instinct, but they also brought urban culture, industriousness, and know-how with them. So did we, and this spirit has not yet died; it is only sleeping. As far back as the 1890s, a few years after the Census Bureau formally eliminated the "frontier line" from its reports, American historian Frederick Jackson Turner wrote that, "He would be a rash prophet who should assert that the expansive character of American life has now entirely ceased. Movement has been its dominant fact, and, unless this training has no effect upon a people, the American energy will continually demand a wide field for its exercise."[48]

We need to learn from the Israelis that "the challenge facing every developed country is to become an idea factory."[49] We need to restore, from our own past, the same adventurous spirit of expansion. This time it is not a physical expansion of territory, but mentally expanding and carrying out our ideas. We have to learn from Shimon Peres, and from ourselves, that the most careful thing is to dare.

FLEXIBILITY: FINDING WHAT WORKS

This section might be entitled "Do what works, not necessarily what you *think* works." Even this apparently logical attitude raises questions—in particular, how do we measure what works?

There is a question of context with government, with appreciating context more often honored in the breech. Many people fear change and automatically rely on the old familiar, especially if the familiar seems to be working. One problem with the American economy has been this desire for the familiar, when it appeared to be working. And one reason the familiar appeared to be on the right track was that it was impossible to measure opportunity cost. By this I mean that the government can accurately measure the number of people who lose their jobs, i.e., the number of people who apply and are on unemployment. They can also measure international corporation hires overseas, and then compare them to employment lost in the same areas in this country. But how can we measure the number of jobs *not created*? We can't.

Cause and effect can truly be measured once the effect has been seen. Even at the start of the Great Recession, with major financial institutions either on the verge of collapse or collapsing, we had a good idea (TARP) but could not know what would happen. Now we know that the economy had become too dependent on fancy financing, and too negligent of actually doing something with all that money. Does doing something necessarily mean producing something? Not always. Actual production of numerous different projects is going to be cheaper overseas, even with shipping back to the United States, for the foreseeable future. Doing something does include, however, creating new products as well as new ways of producing them.

Cause and effect is tricky enough to measure *after* the effect. All experiences occur within a particular context, as do different aspects of life. We cannot always relate cause to effect. Before the effect has happened, it is impossible to measure. For example, let's say a number of businesses are created in an area during a particular period of time. A new tax measure is introduced, raising or lowering the amount due. What happens to business creation (started before the new tax) when the tax has time to take effect? In a large urban setting, such as New York City, it might take even longer to see. The MTA tax, as noted earlier, is not likely to cause businesses to suddenly shut down, or even to break their leases and desert the city. But for those who do leave, will it be because of this tax, or because they found they could work just as effectively and profitably, and more cheaply, in the further upstate suburbs or in another state?

Flexibility is a matter of attitude, of doing the work regardless of its ideological source. Although I am anything but pro-big government and pro-regulation, I saw the need for the bank bailout, TARP, and the first stimulus program. President George W. Bush, a lifelong market conservative, signed off on the first two programs when the alternative was much more dire. And, while the effects of these programs have been mixed, failure to act might well have been catastrophic.

Flexibility on this level should be connected to transparency. To the degree possible, government should always be open and honest about what it is doing and why. Describing the *why* is also a political necessity. How did the Democrats, having taken measures likely necessary to save the economy, do so badly in the 2010 elections? Perhaps by not ensuring that the people knew *why* these measures had been taken and what the alternative would have been. In so doing, they failed to earn either the trust or the benefit of the doubt of the middle twenty percent or so of who decide elections.

Transparency will be beneficial to business and the economy. Imagine what would have happened if the massive, complex system starting with sub-prime mortgages and ending with derivatives based on these mortgages, had come to light a year or two before it did. Perhaps the government would have been motivated to fire a few warning shots to slow things down and get them under control before a global calamity occurred.

Viewed from this perspective, in the future it would be wise to switch to a sane balance between excessive regulation and the reckless free market. Yes, the profit motive has enabled this country to accomplish amazing things. But take elements from both sides of the political spectrum. Recognize (with the Right) that the free market is usually the best way to accomplish things in the economy. Enlightened self-interest is probably the most effective way to grow sections of an economy, and the economy as a whole.

Enlightened self-interest means finding a way to do things which are good for me and also good for you. If I am in the same business as you, I want to compete with you. I want to do better. But I should not—intuitive though it may seem—want to drive you out of business. It can get sloppy when that happens. More importantly, I can make more money if I work to increase the size of my market share. If you are providing a bad product, people will come to me anyway, which increases the level of competition and drives the market forward for me to grow and expand my business. But, if you are providing a good product to the 100 customers for what we make, would I not do better striving for 100 new customers? The answer is obvious.

Government will always have its own unique role. Outside of the few areas everyone agrees upon as its responsibility, such as defense and public safety, government provides something else—an overview of national needs. Government, particularly the federal government, can step in if the private sector goes overboard, as the financial sector did a few years ago. Government can handle new innovations necessary for the country, but not yet profitable. An example of this might be basic research into alternative energies.

Government can even work on a hybrid arrangement for some functions. This concept, discussed in an earlier chapter, has been around for a long time: public-private partnership, frequently called PPP. Each party brings to the table what it does best. Government sets, or approves, goals and looks out for the public interest. The private sector brings its orientation to doing things in a most efficient manner possible.

Citing specific examples does not really define the point of flexibility. The point of flexibility is to carefully monitor and study situations, to spot problems early in the game, and develop solutions, that allows thinking-outside-the-box to become a norm in this evolving economy. The criterion for a solution is that it is likely to work. The watchword is not conservative or liberal, Democratic or Republican, government or private-sector. The watchword is *workable.*

12

THE FUTURE OF SMALL BUSINESSES

FORMING ALLIANCES

Forming alliances with other competitors, affiliates, and associations has an intrinsic value. It broadens your exposure to new markets, while allowing you to access market intelligence and strengthen your brand.

Competitors are in business for one reason: to make money and profit. There are often business opportunities that cannot be handled by one company and there is a need for additional support, or a need to satisfy diversity requirements as stipulated in assigned contracts. Partnerships like this can work when preparing Requests For Proposals (RFPs) from large corporations looking to streamline suppliers and provide fewer contracts. The ability to form agreements like this allows smaller businesses to expand their market platforms and compete with larger suppliers who may have a national or global presence.

While this may seem contradictory, it really isn't. Most small businesses that are service-driven will have to act large in order to remain competitive. The *modus operandi* for future small businesses is to think large and way outside the box. Remaining small is not an option as global competitiveness and the Internet boldly creep through your customers' doors. Consumers large and small are able to get more for less, and this can drive down your profit margins, forcing you to think of new strategies to remain competitive. Many small businesses that service major corporations are forced to vie against national or international competitors. Major corporations prefer giving a single contract to larger suppliers because chances are their presence is global and they're thus able to negotiate better, cheaper contracts with one big supplier, versus several independent smaller suppliers with varying price structures. It is a current trend that will continue into the future. That leaves the small suppliers begging for sub-contracting opportunities from the major supplier. Often this means getting either very little business, or difficult jobs that the major supplier does not want to tackle. So the small business is working twice as hard for half the result, and for a smaller profit margin.

Consider again my idea of small-business clusters. A small business in California that can form an alliance with other small businesses in Florida, Atlanta and New York establishes a foothold in four major regions of the country. This alliance can then compete against a large supplier for that national contract with a major corporation which, on its own, would be impossible for any one of the four to obtain.

Such an alliance will provide a win-win situation for all of the four small businesses involved. Their alliance not only provides an opportunity to compete on a larger scale, covering a broader market, but elevates that alliance to a higher level of competitiveness.

In addition, the possibility of cross-marketing can be an invaluable byproduct of this alliance. One company may have a product or service offering that the other three companies may not possess, allowing that company to cross-sell to established markets within the alliance. This may be the case with other members within the alliance. By agreeing to promote and share in the sale and profit, everyone benefits, the alliance becomes stronger, and its recognition increases.

The benefit to the large corporations goes back to the idea of corporate responsibility. By showing that corporations support small businesses forming cluster alliances to compete on a national or global scale, that corporation sets itself apart from its competitors, provided that the business clusters meet all the necessary quality-assurance benchmarks.

The fear of takeovers and other legal issues can be addressed through the legal process. The structure of the alliance will be outlined, creating laws and bylaws by which it is governed, yet allowing each business owner free rein and control of his or her business.

The small-business clusters will cause you to diversify not only your market share but your product or service offering. For example, you may be an insurance company in Atlanta offering commercial liability insurance as your main service; but what about a geographical region in your alliance where the climate attracts frequent flooding? Offering flood insurance in that region can not only increase your revenue but also allow you to diversify, creating stronger leverage for your company to weather the storm should the primary service offering encounter heavy weather.

MERGERS AND ACQUISITIONS

Mergers and acquisitions are often perceived as a negative step for one business or the other—i.e., a more successful company devouring a weaker one—but it doesn't have to be the case. While there are a number of reasons that small-business owners choose their path, most go into business because they want to make money and/or make a difference in their community. However, as the global economy encroaches on us and profits become smaller due to more competition from competitors both seen and unseen (the Internet), thinking smart is a key step to keeping your company solvent. Merging two small businesses that are logistically strategic or diverse in market share and scope, makes good sense. For example, a business in New York providing Information Technology repair service can seek common ground with a business in Texas providing the sale of computer software. Although they're in the same field, the product/service each offers is different and thus can complement each other by providing an extended market share on both ends.

The key here is to provide a stronger company that captures a diverse and broader market. Growth and expansion is vital to small business success in the future. Remaining isolated on an island only makes your company vulnerable to extinction.

DIVERSIFICATION OF PRODUCTS/SERVICES AND MARKET

"Let's not put all our eggs in one basket, because the basket may have a hole"—a popular saying I've heard often in the past. Diversification is one of the most important principles I learned in business. But I also learned it earlier, on the island where I was born, and from my family. It is as relevant today as it was yesterday, and as it will be tomorrow. Diversification not only allows you to expand the variety of products and services but also to capture a variety of different markets. This becomes crucial when a particular product or service is floundering in a particular market.

For example: my company is located five blocks away from the World Trade Center. The aftereffects of 9/11 were not only devastating emotionally and psychologically, but financially as well. Most of our financial services clients were stagnant for nearly eighteen months, but our medical clients remained active. What did we do? Focused our energy on staffing the medical sector of our business in New York and expanded our operations in our Tampa, Florida office. As a result we were able to ride the difficulties of that time without causing the business to suffer.

In the end we had increased our medical business by sixty-four percent and our Tampa operation doubled in gross revenues.

NETWORKING

One of the keys to a successful business is new-business development. This often involves sales and marketing of your product/service, and has to be a vital and strong component of a business. There are many ways of targeting potential customers: cold calling, referrals, etc. However, in my experience networking is an essential element in growing a business—and networking with the right organizations or groups of people is key.

My best friend, who is also the Vice President of Sales within my company, is a genius at this and has been instrumental in opening doors via networking venues, which she often attends. Being a wallflower doesn't help: you have to be a people-person or hire an individual to represent your company who is unafraid to approach others and make contact. The key to networking successfully is connecting with the right people who can open doors for you, or at least point you in the right direction. Often, it feels like looking for the needle in the proverbial haystack, especially when trying to do business with a large organization. Be bold and ask big questions without fear of intimidation.

Associations like the Chamber of Commerce serve as networking organizations, providing educational forums and corporate sponsors who are accessible to members. There is a wide range of organizations that offer similar services that are invaluable to its members, like the National Minority Business Council, serving the small business community for over forty years. However, these organizations serve an equally important function in this changing economy. They will have to evolve with their members and corporate sponsors in order to provide more value-added services. Otherwise, membership—their key income-earner—will be lost. So their role in the new economy will be to aggressively open doors for members, by providing them with educational information about business trends through workshops and—most importantly—open doors for new-business opportunities that are difficult to access for many small businesses. Hence, reworking the current networking module. On the flip side, corporations are carefully looking at every dollar spent, and for these associations to function effectively in the future economy, they will have to provide an added, measurable value to the corporations to justify their financial support.

INTERNATIONAL TRADE AND SMALL BUSINESS

The future of American small businesses will also rely on how competitive they can remain in a global economy. We have to broaden our horizons beyond the national market to the international. The broader our market scope the more lucrative our business. Therefore, we need to look at international trade as part of the fabric of future small business.

The Internet has brought business from other countries into our homes, lives, smart devices, etc. I received an email this morning from a company in Pakistan wanting to partner with me in providing IT talent. Last week another company wrote to me offering back office support and a 24/7 live receptionist to handle all phone calls. Think of the thousands of foreign companies exporting of goods and services to our country on a regular basis, whether via the Internet or through trading partnerships established here in the US.

The opportunity to trade goods in particular to places like China is becoming the new wave. The Chinese market in particular is very much interested in purchasing goods made in America. This is only one of many international markets that we need to tap into and directly pursue, or they will find larger suppliers here who may be your competitors.

The key to remain successful as a small business in the new, evolving economy is to constantly reinvent your business. There is always something newer and better available, it is your responsibility to figure out what your target market wants and how best to deliver it to them. Companies go out of business because the owners remain inflexible. The ability to move with the ebb and flow of the economy is paramount for your business's survival.

CONCLUSION
The Future

There are six main themes for the book you have almost finished reading. There may be more; that's for you to think about.

THE FIRST THEME is that many of the more serious problems facing the nation during the Great Recession will not automatically vanish when the recession ends.

Spending tax dollars run into the problems of the deficit and national debt. Budget deficits are growing bigger and bigger because we are not producing enough products and services in this country to support a sufficient revenue flow. The bottom line is that we're spending more than we're earning and importing more than we are selling overseas, at the same time that unemployment remains high.

More and more government is being created as we hire people to do the work of government—including work government thinks is necessary to decrease the unemployment rate, however inaccurate such thinking may be. While just about everyone on the political spectrum agrees that some defense spending will always be both obligatory and a necessary function of the federal government, two wars have been devouring billions of dollars.

We can tax citizens more in order to pay for this work. The idea of raising taxes is anathema for government, even before specific taxes are considered. In addition, increasing taxes takes money out of the economy. We are relearning, the hard way, the importance of consumer spending to the economy and to economic recovery. Increasing business taxes takes money that might otherwise be used to hire new employees, especially for small businesses. The new healthcare reform will be an undue burden for small businesses that may have to streamline staff or reconsider hiring new employees as they adjust to this new regulation. Business owners feel they have less money to spend on new employees, and may be even be forced out of state (or the country) for better tax breaks.

The seeming second alternative is to borrow more money, increasing the yearly deficit and the continuing national debt. This might seem the better alternative, as debt has tended to be a safer political alternative to taxes, though this is changing. Governments can also handle a higher debt load than individuals or companies, though there are limits.

The long-term danger of the national debt, and of the deficit, comes when money, as was noted earlier on, behaves like a commodity. When the federal government needs to borrow more money, it decreases the amount available to lend to companies, where it might be used to help create jobs. This is what has happened in the last year or so. Banks, burned by the recession, overcompensated for their former easy virtue by suddenly playing hard to get. Excessive federal borrowing also raises the cost of borrowing. More federal money has to go for debt servicing, rather than for potentially highly valuable federal programs.

These problems augur negatively for economic development, and for a full recovery from the Great Recession.

THE SECOND THEME is that people want their money's worth from taxes, as with any other expenditure. Taxes must be fair, and sensibly spent. People become angry when tax dollars are wasted with little or no accountability. This is why earmarks and set-asides, though a tiny portion of the federal budget, attract such public outrage—at least from the public not directly benefiting from the set-asides. (A "set-aside for small business" is the keeping of an acquisition exclusively for participation by small-business concerns, and a small-business set-aside may be open to all small businesses.)

Set-asides gain media attention—in much the same way that $500 military hammers got far more media attention, and more public ire, than the military paying $40,000,000 for fighter planes that should have cost "only" $20,000,000.

THE THIRD UNDERLYING THEME of this book has been the need for a balanced role for government. The United States federal government has spent a long time being negligent—a strong but justified term—in its dealings with big business, particularly with financial firms engaged in complex financial operations. (Making cars is a lot easier to understand than trading derivative bonds.) Eastern Europe from 1920 through 1989 demonstrated the result of too much regulation and control of the economy. Now the Great Recession has shown us what too *little* regulation and control can bring. Of course, we had already learned this in 1893 and 1929, but while history is long, memory is short. A center course must be determined, and followed.

THE FOURTH THEME is the restoration of economic uniqueness to this country. What can we offer that no one has? I have argued that the most promising area is that of new inventions and new ways of doing things. The responsibility falls on our shoulders as Americans to make this country great by taking bold risks. Government must step out of our way so that we can bloom and prosper. What could be more appropriate, in light of the fact that the United States itself was an invented and self-determined country, taking root in hostile territory?

THE BOOK'S FIFTH THEME is that big business has a vital role to play in what we call social responsibility. In other words, don't outsource goods and services (American jobs) to foreign countries, then import them back to the US. It's almost like pulling the rug from under your own feet. At some point large corporations have to be mindful of our environment, the society in which they serve and their responsibility as big businesses to ensure that the smaller businesses aren't going to vanish. Profit is the goal of every major corporation but at what point do you balance profit and responsibility to form a healthy balance?

THE SIXTH THEME, perhaps the most important, is that our focus should have been, and in the future must be, on small business. This is the fount of the advances, technical and economic, that will restore our economic leadership role in the world.

While small business is the focus of my ideas for long-term economic recovery, we will need to pursue other areas as they become apparent. And in helping business, we will need to use a different means of approach. We will need to catch them before they fail, as with Danielle's PR firm. An excess of such failings accounts for the high unemployment now being experienced.

A recent history of the sub-prime mortgage crisis summarized the role of Wall Street in the economy, and what the role has been and should be.

> *Throughout most of the high-tech era of the last part of the twentieth century, the wizards of Wall Street were justifiably proud of the role they had come to play in providing venture capital to entrepreneurs. The ability of a smart person with a smart idea to turn it into a new company and new product in the United States was unmatched in the world. It was the heart of America's strength, and it was thanks in good part to the rollicking open market in Wall Street.*
>
> *But somewhere along the line, toward the end of this era—as the zeitgeist hit its peak and government regulators backed off completely—Wall Street became the master of Main Street rather than its handmaiden. Wall Street turned ordinary CEOs into stock watchers worried mainly about*

the performance of their options, and tied corporate time horizons to the upticks and downticks of the stock market. Venture capitalism transmogrified into speculative fever.[50]

Some firms on Wall Street grew too big to fail, when the inevitable result of recklessness occurred. Questionable investments backed by questionable loans, despite apparent short-term success, were not the way to create a lasting, stable economic society.

The immediate focus, as has been explained earlier, had to be on the large corporations, banks, and investors, before they dragged the country—and the world—into an even worse disaster than had already occurred. This was a necessary first action, to stop the economic ship from sinking. But now it is time to move on. We have to create an economic and regulatory précis for big business that:

- Encourages social and environmental responsibility.
- Provides guidance.
- Does not allow behavior that can endanger society.
- Prevents damage but does not restrict innovation.

This will require a more consistent, monitored balance, not volatile swings from pillar to post.

Specific regulatory actions, except for those supporting transparency, should be minimized. With freedom of information ranking as a major government principle,

I see the best regulatory approach as the domestic, economic version of Cold War deterrence. The existence of nuclear weapons ensured rational behavior on the part of the superpowers and their main allies, while—minus a few close calls—never being used.

While smaller business should be the focus of the bulk of government assistance, this signifies more than simply ordering small business with regard to what they must or must not do. Government needs to function as a source of technical guidance and information for business, as explained in earlier chapters; and make it easier for businesses to gain the information they need to start, and to thrive. Even before examining regulations for necessity, even before cutting back on the American "regulatory raj," we must centralize requirements for business. Establish one-stop shopping for requirements and regulations, so businesses can concentrate on what they do best: doing business.

A major role of government is to create an environment in which business can be innovate and thrive. America's strength has traditionally been born out from the ability of one person with a brilliant idea for a new product, and a new company to sell the product. We have only to think of Henry Ford. Encouraging innovation is playing to our greatest strength—our can-do spirit—and the surest path to restore and secure our leading place in the world.

Can things ever be "normal" again after the upheaval of the Great Recession? Think how much more we can become if we work to bring out the creative ability of more Americans—how much better than "normal." We can do this by not just encouraging people to create ideas, but by helping them determine what ideas are viable, and assisting in their ultimate production.

Assisting small business requires close examination of regulations to determine which ones are needed, and which exist simply because they always have. A truly bipartisan effort is essential in appraising whether the benefits of the regulations outweigh the costs of compliance. In many ways a regulation is like an investment—something from which maximum return must be sought.

My own experience echoes that of thousands. Making no judgment on the need for the particular regulations I had to meet when expanding my business to other states across the nation, the red tape and bureaucracy made it more challenging and complex than necessary. A centralized business online service would have made all the difference, both time-wise and financially. This would improve the climate for entrepreneurs, both by positive incentives—direction to funding—and by removing obstructions, or at least letting the perspective businessperson identify what the roadblocks are, where they are located, and how to efficiently surmount them.

The focus of this book has been on small business, where job-creation is highest, as the best way to encourage economic growth. Most people will not desire relocation to another location. The main reason I opened my business in New York is that I already lived here. Human nature generally dictates staying in the place where one has roots, rather than moving to a completely new area, but in the age of technology those sentiments are rapidly changing.

One possible argument against my ideas for one-stop centers is that they will cause states to compete with each other. A business that moves from New York to Maryland, for example, helps Maryland, but hurts New York. People will merely compare regulations and requirements in both states and make their decisions accordingly. But jobs, some may argue, are thus being created in Maryland at New York State's expense.

Well, it's already happening, and at a faster rate than reported. Leveling the competitive edge of each state allows for better government management of their particular geographical region by proactively attending to the subtle changes in the economy and thereby making subtle course corrections, as opposed to a late reaction to a situation when the signs were flashing *danger* all along. New York will always be a desirable place for companies to have a presence, due to the positive brand engendered by the state. However, it's up to the government to ensure that the brand isn't tarnished by high taxes and overregulation, or perceived as *anti-* rather than *pro-*business.

Although unlikely, I don't think it would be so bad if state business regulations became relatively uniform. States will always have particular geographical or technological advantages. These can be natural, such as Arizona having more sun for solar power production than Maine. Or they may result from the regional economic centers, such as Silicon Valley or its counterparts in Utah and the Boston area. The main point is not *where* in the United States innovation, entrepreneurship, and job growth are encouraged, but that they *are* encouraged.

The vital element is to create a climate where people not only can succeed, but believe they can succeed...a climate in which they will be willing to try, which also accepts failure and encourages innovators and entrepreneurs to try again. We can learn from other countries, but we can better seek out our own strengths, and adapt to our own circumstances.

FINAL THOUGHTS TO TAKE AWAY

It is worth a review of the basic points covered throughout this book. To wit: The economic realities of the 21st century are here to stay. Not only should we not hide from them, we must meet them head on. Either the Great Recession can be seen as the economic tragedy of our time, or we can use it as an opportunity to rebuild our nation stronger and better than before. Out of every misfortune lies an opportunity to start anew and create a miracle.

The United States of America was founded by people with vision, but evolved on account of innovative minds, hard work, and determination. Over the centuries since its inception, we have survived panics, depressions, and recessions galore, bouncing back every time. This time, the stakes are higher and the global playing field has changed dramatically. But the ideas outlined in *One Hundred Pennies* have, I hope, put things into perspective. Understanding the true value of one hundred pennies in relation to our economy allows us to say that encouraging invention and proactively supporting small businesses is where the strength of the U.S. economy lies. With decisive action taken by bringing government, big and small businesses to the table, working cohesively to solve our problems, we are guaranteed to shine a light on the pathway out of our approaching future and into a far better one.

ENDNOTES

1. SBA.gov
2. SBA.gov
3. The New Republic, "Waste Land" by Gregg Easterbrook. November 10, 2010
4. New York Times 5/14/11
5. Testimony of Dr. Alan Greenspan, Committee of Government Oversight and Reform October <http://clipsandcomment.com/wp-content/uploads/2008/10/greenspan-testimorny-20081023pdf>
6. Tocqueville, Alexis de. *Democracy in America*. Chicago: University of Chicago Press, 2000; p. 647
7. Segal, Adam. *Advantage: How American Innovation Can Overcome the Asian Challenge*. New York. W.W. Norton & Co, 2011; pp. 41-48
8. Segal, pp 61-62
9. Middlekauff, Robert. *The Glorious Cause: The American Revolution 1763-1789*. New York. Oxford University Press. 2005. p. 3
10. Middlekauff p. 685
11. Stiglitz, Joseph. *The Roaring Nineties: A New History of the World's Most Prosperous Decade*. New York. W.W. Norton & Co, 2003, p. 159
12. Hirsh, Michael. *Capital Offense: How Washington's Wise Man Turned America's Future Over to Wall Street*. Hoboken, N.J. John C. Wiley & Sons, Inc. 2010. p. 61
13. Hirsh, p. 183
14. Hudson, Michael W. The Monster: How a Gang of Predatory Lenders and Wall Street Bankers Fleeced America and Spawned a Global Crisis. New York: Times Books, Henry Holt & Co. 2010. p. 281
15. Hudson (page not given)
16. http://smallbusiness.aol.com/2011/06/01/kim-and-scotts-gourmet-pretzels-a-new-twist-on-success/
17. New York State Department of Labor. "New York State's Economy Added 700 Private Sector Jobs in November." December 16, 2010, <http://www.labor.ny.gov/stats/pressreleases/pruistat.shtm>
18. Bureau of Labor Statistics, United States Dept. of Labor. "The Employment Situation, November 2010," December 3, 2010 <www.bls.gov/new.release/pdf/empsit.pdf>
19. HRM Guide, Human Resources Management, "UK Unemployment, Labour Market Statistics, December 15, 2010. www.hrmguide.co.uk/jobmarket/umemployment.htm
20. Steffy, Loren C. *Drowning in Oil: BP and the Reckless Pursuit of Profit*. New York: McGraw Hill, 2011

21. U.S. Dept. of Commerce, December 10, 2010 "U.S. International Trade in Goods and Services." www.census.gov/foreign-trade/Press-Release/current_press_release/ft900.pdf
22. AFL-CIO "Exporting America" 2010. www.aflcio.org/issues/jobseconomy/exportingamerica/outsourcing_problems.cfm
23. ibid
24. ibid
25. "The Hackett Group: Acceleration of Offshoring Trend Driving Loss of Millions of Finance and IT Jobs in U.S. and Europe." www.thehackettgroup.com/about/alerts/alerts_2010/alert_120220.jsp
26. Computer World UK, "Businesses Disappointed with Quality of Offshore Work," March 23, 2010. www.networkworld.com/news/2010/032410-businesses-disappointed-with-quality-of.html
27. Bergreen, Laurence. *Marco Polo: From Venice to Xanadu*, New York: Alfred A. Knopf, 2007. p. 127
28. 1010WINS, February 14, 2011
29. Hirsh, p. 36
30. Hirsh, pp. 1, 3, 64, 218-219
31. Headd, Brian, SBA, Office of Advocacy, "An Analysis of Small Business and Jobs," March 2010. www.sba.gov/
32. Headd, p. 7
33. Headd, p. 11
34. Headd, p. 3
35. Headd, p. 6
36. Headd, p. 14
37. Drucker, Peter, Innovation and Entrepreneurship. New York: HarperCollins 1985, p. 19
38. King, Steve and Ockets, Carolyn. "Research Brief: Defining Small Business Innovation," March 2009. http://download.intuit.com/
39. Eckfiled, Richard and Brager, Bruce L., "Cities as Energy Producers: The Report of the United States Conference of Mayors, European Task Force," Washington, DC: U.S. Conference of Mayors January 15, 1982, pp. 40-51
40. Inslee and Hendreicks, pp. 251-252, 270
41. Berg, Jon E. and Monroe, Marsha C. "Waste-to-Energy Program" Wood Energy Case Study, Cooperative Extension Service, University of Florida, Institute of Food and Agricultural Services. September 2007
42. Center for an Urban Future, p.14
43. Center for an Urban Future, p. 15
44. Center for an Urban future, p. 18
45. Dan Senor and Saul Singer, *The Story of Israel's Economic Miracle*, New York: Twelve, Hachette Book Group, quoted p. 209
46. Senor and Singer, p. 19
47. www.mahal-idf-volunteers.org/inofrmation/background/content.htm
48. Frederick Jackson Turner, *The Frontier in American History*, Tucson and London: The University of Arizona Press, 1986 reprint of 1920 edition, p. 37
49. Senor and Singer, p. 235
50. Hirsh, p. 20

CPSIA information can be obtained at www.ICGtesting.com
Printed in the USA
BVOW071335160113

310341BV00002B/2/P